THE REALITY BEHIND THE GLAMOUR OF COLLEGE ATHLETICS

D1601247

BY: ACHEIL TAC

Editing by Arlene Dagadu, and James Ebert.

Cover design by Mithun Miah.

Printed in the United States of America

Dedication Page

To my dearest friend, sister, and teammate Eboniey Jeter: I'm sorry that life in college wasn't what you expected and life for you ended way too soon. I am sorry your mental state was not protected as much as it should have been. I should have done more. Every day I regret not doing more.

You were so full of life and after freshman year, I knew you were going to be my person. I survived college due to your genuine friendship and support to keep me focused. I hope you forgive me for not knowing and not being there for you when you needed my friendship and support most. I hope you are where there is peace and love. I hope you have arrived at a place where love overflows and where the ball never stops bouncing. Your spirit lives on forever in my heart because you are an individual who is hard to forget. Because of you, I can help others and inspire others as you have inspired me. I love you. I miss you. Please continue to watch over me.

"Fly High 5"

Preface

This book was written during a time in my life when I was going through a severe injury that forced me to be truly alone with my own thoughts and figure out who I was and what my next steps were in my journey. The opportunity to be a professional athlete caused me to reflect on college athletics and the journey I took to get to where I was, and now am. I never in my 25 years of life thought I would ever become a writer, let alone an author. This journey is interesting, stressful, enriching, life-changing, inspiring, and rewarding all in one.

College for me was interesting for its life-changing education, but more interesting due to the number of athletes I connected with and met along the way. It is crazy to think that fifteen plus athletes who are put on a team without initially knowing each other, who are forced to get along due to the sport they play, will end up valuing each other more than they thought they would. The way in which athletes look at college and live through college is much different than someone who isn't or was never a college athlete.

Many people have opinions and misconceptions of what college life is like for athletes and what we go through. They think having a scholarship is the greatest thing in the world and life is a breeze after that. While receiving a scholarship is a blessing, the payment for that is not only taxing on an athlete's mind but body as well. We struggle to juggle many things during our transitional period from being just students in high school playing a sport, to emerging as adults in college playing at the highest level of competition.

I was also inspired and motivated by the younger generation of athletes going through the process. Some do not understand the system and how it operates, starting from the recruitment process and all the way to retirement from the athletic arena. There is this path drawn out for us that we take advantage of, but never look past or above. This pre-destined journey that you are supposed to take as an athlete if you want to truly be successful within your sport and in life.

The only fault we entertain is not wanting more for ourselves and only tying ourselves to one identity growing up. Due to this, we struggle to find ourselves and our purpose outside of sports when our playing days end.

The purpose of this book is not to tell you what to do, bash any institution, or persuade you one way or another. The purpose is to inspire athletes to be more than what they see themselves as, encourage the academic aspect of college athletics, voice the importance of mental health in athletes, and present and enlighten the minds of athletes with facts and information that were not entirely at their disposal before.

The process of authoring this book was not only difficult but exhausting because I wanted to communicate the information clearly and effectively. I started writing in March of 2018 and changed the release date so many times because I thought it was not ready. I reached out to various people that I thought could pour life into this work and most agreed and invested, while others never came through. To those that believed and invested, I am forever grateful and to those that did not see the vision initially, I hope you see it now.

I hope you learn valuable information and are inspired to apply it to your own life. Throughout the book, you will hear from various athletes at various levels of competition speak their truth and past experiences. I hope that the principles discussed in this book are a blessing and are useful and beneficial to you and others.

Introduction

College is an educational institute that not only provides life-changing education for its students but also life changing experiences. College is a place of self-discovery, identity formation, and a place that creates connections that last a lifetime.

Athletes in college sports gain a valuable education as well as a life learning experience. Athletes compete in college sports for many reasons. These reasons may include but are not limited to love of the sport, a way to shift focus and keep themselves out of trouble and pursue something meaningful, a path to go professional and make money to take care of their families in the future, or an opportunity to gain an education that would have otherwise been difficult and hard to obtain without a scholarship.

For those reasons and many others, athletes at an early age dedicate their childhoods chasing athletic scholarships so that they may have the opportunity to fulfill their future needs and desires. When they finally obtain that scholarship and enter the college athletic world, most quickly find that just having a scholarship is not enough and they end up wanting more. The problem is, the only thing they are ever guaranteed through these athletic scholarships is a degree of their choice during their years of competition.

The National Collegiate Athletic Association (NCAA) which brings the college athletic world together, is a non-profit, tax-exempt organization that governs and regulates college athletic competition as well as their coaches and the athletes that compete in these sports. Their job is to oversee and provide rules and regulations on what athletes can and cannot do as well as what an athletic program can and cannot do or provide their athletes during their period of eligibility.

Per NCAA rules, athletes are not allowed to get compensation for their athletic work on the field or court and are not able to obtain work during the season due to the demands of their sport. They must remain amateurs during their years of competition. If they ever violate the rules and regulations put in place by the institution and the NCAA, they are at risk of suspension from competition as well as at risk of losing their scholarships altogether.

What happens after an athlete receives a scholarship is never discussed or examined. Most outsiders believe that being an athlete is a simple job and that receiving a scholarship to compete in their sports is a gift and that athletes are ungrateful should they ever want more for themselves. According to the NCAA and others who oppose pay for athletes, the thought of compensating athletes for their work should never be a topic of discussion. Athletes at the college level are viewed as amateurs and should remain at that status until they graduate and go on to compete at the professional level.

It is also believed that getting a free education should be enough and a motivating factor for athletes because it is something most young persons do not have the opportunity to obtain. Athletes are judged only through their athletic identity and never looked at as more than that identity.

They are taken advantage of at times and never given the proper education promised to them because certain athletic programs brainwash athletes into thinking their sport is the most important thing. This in turn gives the athlete the idea that academics should follow and take a backseat to athletics. Some athletes are motivated and determined to use their athletic ability to get to the professional world. Told that they should only focus on their sport rather than their academics and sports, they will most likely shift their focus on excelling in their sport.

There are athletes that come from nothing and try to make something out of their situations by using their athletic skills to achieve future success. Because college athletes cannot work or receive support from their coaching staff, there are times when an athlete will have no food or even money to help support them. According to NCAA rules, coaches are not able to help buy food or other necessities of life for athletes as it would violate the NCAA rules.

Some athletes will have mental and physical breakdowns or even get burned out from their sport and school. Injuries might happen and when they do, some have a hard time coping and dealing with the possibility of sitting out an entire year or the thought of their careers possibly ending due to the severity of their injuries. To an athlete, the thought of their sport ending is a tough pill to swallow. It is an even bigger eye opener when athletes finally realize the importance of their education in the reality of life after college.

In the 1950s, the NCAA coined the term "student-athlete" to help remind athletes that they are amateurs and not professionals. The troubling thing about this term is that the NCAA makes it seem as if they value an athlete's education, but what is truly valued of the athlete is their athletic abilities and the amount of money they can provide the school through competition. It has been proven time and time again that the NCAA and most college athletic programs are not too concerned with the grades a student athlete is making in the class or what degree path they are pursuing, if they maintain their eligibility status and meet the bare minimum that is required of them in the classroom so that they are able to compete and graduate in a timely manner. Some athletes put their educational responsibilities into someone else's hands and fail to take control themselves.

They let their advisors, coaches, and even sometimes their teammates dictate what degree path they should pursue. Though they cannot be compensated for their work, athletes are held to a certain standard, put on a certain time constraint, and expected to achieve success both in their sport and in the classroom. Expectations are set high for the athletes both by the NCAA, the university, coaches, teammates, and professors.

The life of a college student-athlete is often most glamorized by outsiders looking in. What most people do not realize is that athletes live three different lives in college, and often struggle to balance all three, take care of themselves, and remain focused. Athletes strain themselves to maintain their student lives, their athletic lives, and their social lives, as well as maintain a certain image for the outsiders scrutinizing them.

They are placed on a pedestal and are expected to satisfy the needs and expectations of the public as well as their peers. They are only supported due to their athletic ability, and if they ever fall short of such, supported less or even overlooked.

With these expectations, athletes are likely to undergo a multitude of stressors regarding their education and their sport and sometimes their personal lives as well. Examples of these stressors include but are not limited to mental or psychological stress, physical stress, emotional stress, social stress, and sometimes, financial stress. If experienced severely and very often, these stressors can cause serious problems and damage to the student athletes' mental state, confidence level and self-worth.

It is imperative that we educate, prepare, and advise our athletes of what it truly means to be a student-athlete. We need to speak truth, mentor, and give realistic advice as well as show them a glimpse of the student-athletic life. Although the college athletic system isn't perfect and most definitely needs work and a great deal of change in how they treat their student athletes, it is up to the student athletes in the meantime to find their voice and encourage themselves to take their education seriously and find ways to cope with situations they might be dealing with and take a stand.

If athletes do not take themselves seriously, others won't take them seriously. To fight for what you are missing and needing, you already must be taking advantage of what is given. Change does not start with them, change starts with you and then you can demand it of them. There is always a reality to every perceived glamour.

TABLE OF CONTENTS

CHAPTER 1

Egypt to America

Being born in South Sudan, a war-torn country and moving to Egypt, sports were not a thing for me to focus on or pursue. In Sudan, what was stressed most, even today, was educational freedom. They believed and still believe that education provides more opportunities than your parents or this world could ever grant you without it. Growing up, my parents did not have the same educational opportunities I have now. They got married at an early age and dedicated their lives to taking care of my sisters and me and ensuring that we have a better life and future than they did.

My Dad graduated from high school and college in South Sudan and was a teacher of mathematics in Egypt. He was a very smart man who had intense, mathematical brain power. My Mom did not complete high school and never had the opportunity to go back and finish. Due to such circumstances, my parents stressed the importance of education. They taught us how education helps you live a free life as well as give you whatever it is you were trying to get out of life.

They always said education is something that nobody could ever take away from you. Education gives you awareness and allows you to be able to understand the world around you and impact it in a significant way. It is something that will be with you forever. It is the key to success. While education might be free for some, costly for others, and often hard to obtain overall, it provides opportunities, fulfills dreams, and provides a sense of accomplishment.

Growing up in Egypt, my parents believed the educational institution was not up to par and did not align with their career aspirations for us, so they decided to move to America. When we arrived, I was nine years old. There are four girls in my family including myself. I am the eldest of the Tac sisters. The good thing about the move was my uncle was already living here and was able to help with the transition and made sure we understood the American system and how it all worked.

I was registered in school and placed in the third grade. The concern with placement was that I was too old to start over in kindergarten to learn the language, and very foreign and behind to start in the third grade. My parents decided that they were certainly not going to start me in kindergarten at nine years old and took their chances with me in the third grade.

The school offered to also place me in an additional class termed English as a Second Language (ESL) to help with my transition and catch me up to speed with kids my age. ESL provides foreign kids the opportunity to gain more knowledge outside of their classes and help them catch up with the rest of the kids. School was tough and making friends was tougher.

I didn't know any English and communication was technically nonexistent. I felt like a child needing to relearn everything from the beginning. The only languages I knew at the time were Arabic and Dinka, which were what I spoke at home.

I remember one day in class, my teacher asked me to print my name on the board because she thought it was interesting. I got up, shy as ever, and went to the board. I did not know how to write in English at the time let alone speak the language, so I printed my name in Arabic. Coming from Egypt, they mostly taught us Arabic and the only English we learned were the easy, basic words that you could not even use to form a sentence.

When I wrote in Arabic, I can guarantee you everyone there was confused. Instead of making a big deal out of it, my teacher thanked me and pointed me to my seat.

I will never forget that event because it helped me realize how far I've come in life. Sometimes in life, we as human beings focus a lot on what is ahead and what the future holds. We never pause to think where we are and reflect on our journey and how far we've come. I believe that pausing sometimes in life can help you move forward when you seem to be stuck in the present.

You can't change your past by any means, but you can use it to measure how far you've come, help you realize where you are, and help direct you into your next path in life.

 Being in a foreign country, it took a while to adjust and learn the culture. The American culture was different from the African culture I was used to. The food tasted different, people dressed differently, communication was different, and the overall environment was new.

Since it was hard making friends, I would go home after school and watch TV. You are probably asking yourselves, why is she watching TV when this girl does not know English? Well, TV shows helped me learn the language. For entertainment, I would watch WWE RAW. RAW is a professional wrestling television program that every African becomes obsessed with when coming to the States.

I would also watch soap operas such as "Days of Our Lives" and "The Young and the Restless". Although it didn't make

3

much sense at the time, the shows helped me gain an understanding of what was going on. They both helped me learn English and also taught me the American culture.

Generally speaking, when you are a foreigner who already speaks a different language, it is easier for you to learn a second language. Over time, things began feeling normal and fitting in was not so hard to do anymore. A couple of years flew by and my Mom and Dad ended up separating. My mother was then left to take care of four young girls alone. Due to the separation, we moved around with our Mom a lot. I experienced inconsistency in my life regarding schooling, going from school to school. I tried making friends wherever we went, but after a while it all seemed pointless.

I remember when I tried out for the sixth-grade basketball middle school team at Lake Highlands Middle School. I only tried out because my friends were going out for the team and they convinced me to do so as well. I was very skinny, short, shaped like a twig and a very uncoordinated kid.

I did not get my height until about my eighth-grade year in middle school. I tried out and ended up not making the team. Although it hurt that I did not make the team and my friend did, it didn't stop me from doing other sports. I played soccer and I ran track, which I was exceptionally good at, but I ended up hating it because of all the running I had to do.

Today, I still feel like anything where running is involved is a punishment and not a sport. I still have PTSD from all the running I was forced to do in high school and college. Every day in practice that we had to run without the ball in our hands for conditioning or punishment, I would stop and ask myself, is this really what you want to do with your life? Do you want to try volleyball instead? The only people who probably will not relate to this are track runners. Their career and purpose are to run. It takes a brave soul to dedicate their entire childhood and college years to running. You guys are truly the real MVPs.

Going into my seventh-grade year, we moved again. I knew at some point I wanted to try basketball once more. The sport fascinated me after my tryout session in sixth grade, and I wanted to see if I could make the seventh-grade team. The fascination came from the creativity, freedom, and versatility of the game. Anyone at any time can impact the game negatively or positively, and just like any other sport, you need your team completely involved to be able to win.

During PhyEd (PE) class one day, I asked the coach if he knew about tryouts. He informed me that they had tryouts the previous year and did not hold tryouts until the end of the year. I was devastated, but I stayed in PE like any other normal kid and chose to play recreational basketball every day.

I didn't play the sport outside of PE. I never had any skill work with trainers, never watched it on TV, never knew what the official rules were. I was basically going blindly into the situation.

When the first year of high school came, I decided to try out once more for the team. What I did not know was, if you were a good enough player, they offered you a free scholarship to college to get your bachelor's degree. The professional world after college was also a mystery to me. It is safe to say, I was clueless about the sport and the world in which it was played.

I remember all four years of my high school experience so vividly. My first year, I made the freshman team and I was so bad that my freshman coach would only start me to tip the ball and then bench me. During my comfortable time on the bench,

I was learning and picking up things. I paid attention to everything the coach was saying and what the kids were doing.

I remember one game clearly because something clicked in my brain and my body and I finally got the concept of basketball. The girls from the other team were talking a lot of trash the whole game and I was just fed up.

I wanted to get on the court, block their shots and do the Mutombo "no no no" in their faces. I think it was my anger and annoyance that made me want to put myself out there, do my best, and try to win for my teammates.

I am an extremely fast learner, especially visually. So, if you demonstrate something exactly how you want it done, I can do it and that's how basketball was for me. In practice, coach would tell us what he wanted us to run, demonstrate it visually and surely enough, I was doing it.

Sophomore year came around, and I got moved up to Junior Varsity (JV). What a big world it seemed at the time. While players played Amateur Athletic Union (AAU) basketball and had trainers working on their skill sets during the summer, I was at home at the street hoop shooting kids buckets daily. That's mostly how I spent my summers. I was not informed about AAU basketball and I didn't know anything about connecting with trainers or anything.

Basketball at this point was just a hobby that I loved doing. I was not thinking of future plans or goals. I didn't even know at the time basketball would become my future. Sophomore year on JV went well. My skills got much better, and coach even started noticing my growth as a player, teammate, and leader. She trusted me with more responsibilities on the team. The expectations for the team and me were set high, as they should have been.

My junior year, I got moved up to varsity. I technically got moved up after my JV season ended and varsity made it into playoffs. They moved a couple of us up just in case their players fouled out and they needed extra bodies to play. Unfortunately, our varsity team at the time did not win their playoff game. We had the opportunity to play for a couple of minutes towards the end of the game after the varsity girls came out of the game. If you know basketball, or were a player at the time, you know girls were monsters back in the day.

They were athletic, fast, aggressive, and overall incredibly competitive. They had that raw talent, and it was fascinating to witness in high school. I never imagined myself playing or even competing with girls of that nature at the time. It was scary but an interesting, growth opportunity and experience.

As I continued to get better and better, my coaches increasingly relied on me to produce and win games. I obviously had teammates that helped with this process, but a lot of stress was put on me to perform to the best of my abilities and win games.

I remember playing one of our district games and having to guard their best point guard. I am a forward/center, but I was long, fast, and athletic enough to guard point guards, as well as other players that played positions outside of the paint. The problem was not in guarding the point guard herself. The problem came from not having the opportunity to create scoring opportunities for my teammates and score for myself. Most of the time, I would get doubled guarded and would not get the opportunity to score.

It frustrated me. Here I was working hard on defense to

prevent one of their best players from scoring, and they were doing the same thing to me. More frustration came from my coaches expecting me to find a way to score, then the other team doubling me. The pressure and the stress of that game caused me to shut down completely.

When I was playing in high school and even my early college years, when things did not go my way, I had a bad habit of shutting down completely and not being able to come back from it. It got to the point where my coach had to take me out of the game to talk to me and help me get my mind right again. It was not purposely done; I just always set high expectations for myself and expected to be perfect that when I fell short of those expectations, frustration overwhelmed me, and I shut down.

Coaches should know when an athlete is shutting down, it is not because they are being selfish and not getting their way. It is because they want to win and are struggling to perform. Coaches should know how to handle their players to get the best performance out of them. My coach was remarkably familiar with my personality and understood how to address me in that situation to get the best athlete out of me in that moment. She did not yell at me to make it worse. She just simply told me what she expected me to do, that my teammates had my back, and that I didn't need to do everything myself.

Oftentimes as athletes, we think that since so much is put on us, that we must save the day. The best thing to do in those situations is to have your teammates help you out. If you are struggling to perform, it is good to rely on your teammates to help pick up some of the load that you might be struggling to carry. She talked to me, gave me some pointers, and sent me back on the court.

Although varsity competition was a little tough, my teammates made the experience a great one. We were all aware of our roles, and we played them well. Coaches should not limit players by any means but, players should also be aware of their own skill sets. If rebounding is what you do best, and it impacts the team in a positive light, then that's what you need to do come game time. This is not to say you can never change roles and suddenly take on a different role. For the sake of playing time, which concerns every athlete that plays sports, find something you do exceptionally well and do that. Also, be willing to work on those weak skills that you might have and over time turn them into your strengths.

I remember playing with my point guard Candice Followwell in high school. She played varsity all four years of her high school career, so she was more experienced than most of us. I am going to be honest, she was the best point guard I have ever had, and I'll tell you why. As a point guard, your job is to set your teammates up for success in their perspective positions.

You are the ringleader of the show, and you should be aware of your teammates' weaknesses and strengths. She was very much aware and always knew where I needed the ball the most to be effective. She read me so well that I literally did not have to second guess when she was throwing it, where she was throwing it, or how she was throwing it.

We had a connection on the court that a point guard and center aspire to have on any team. Her main goal was not to get her points, steals or assists. Her main goal every time she stepped on the court was to win and make sure we all did our jobs to secure that win. She was a great leader and although we had our differences at times on the court, she pushed us to bring the best out of us. Because of this and the relationship and chemistry our team had, we went undefeated and became district champions.

We also had the opportunity to make it to the elite eight in the playoffs before our season was cut short. Even though our season ended too soon, the run was an incredible one and the memories of that 2012 team will live on forever in my heart.

It was not until after my junior year in high school that I found out about AAU basketball. Teams started reaching out to me, wanting me to play for them. I did not know anything about AAU basketball other than the fact that athletes played to keep in shape during the summer as well as sharpen their skills and get exposure. I committed to a team that two of my high school teammates played on. I wanted to compete with people that were familiar with my playing style and knew me personally.

Athletes today know what teams they should play for and what teams they shouldn't to get the greatest amount of exposure. Back then, we didn't have those concerns. We picked a team to play for and tried winning every tournament, so we could play in bigger tournaments and travel. The way AAU basketball is designed today is different than how it was when I was growing up in the sport.

Parents spend a lot of money nowadays to provide their kids with the best trainers and gear to place them on the best AAU teams possible. They provide their kids with the greatest amount of exposure.

AAU basketball has grown as well, leaving many high school coaches with less control over athletes and their recruiting process. College coaches are recruiting more through AAU coaches and athletes have noticed, leading them to search for the best AAU programs.

As a parent, I would want to put my child on the best AAU program to get exposure and I would spend the money, time, and effort it took to provide my child the best experience ever. Parents should keep in mind   that not all athletes will be eligible to receive scholarships to college.

The probability of competing beyond high school for some is slim. It was reported that nearly 8 million student athletes currently participate in high school athletics and out of that 8 million, only 480,000 will get the opportunity to compete at NCAA schools. Only a fraction of the 480,000 will attain their goals of playing professional in the league or the Olympics.

My advice is, you can invest in your child all you want but at the end of the day, coaches make their decisions on who they want to attend and play for their athletic programs as well as their university.

If your child is talented, they will get seen. If you want to develop your child, hiring a trainer is not always the first solution. Most of today's athletes lack basic skills and knowledge of their sport. They lack the fundamentals of the sport but are eager to learn how to make moves that they will probably never even use in a game or even practice.

There arc athletes that train with trainers all year but lack the confidence when it is game time to use the skills taught to them by trainers to help them compete and win games. For athletes to reach their full potential, they must learn the fundamentals of their sport, have the knowledge and intelligence it requires, and then sharpen their skills as they go. You cannot get better and build if you have not laid down the basics and learned the fundamentals.

Joining an AAU team during the summer felt like I entered a new world, and people were just noticing me for the first time. They noticed my height, my abilities, and the potential for the kind of player I could become. But that's usually how college coaches scout anyway.

They scout potential, and what they can do with that potential. I went through the entire recruiting process with no awareness of how the process all worked, and my high school coach was just as clueless as I was for the most part.

I took notes and advice from the college coaches who were recruiting me. They mentioned that applying for school was a necessity and that you did not just get accepted into college because you were offered an athletic scholarship. Taking the SAT or ACT achievement test was necessary, and your grade point average was an important part of getting accepted into school.

These are important things that some high school athletes and coaches are not aware of that affect the athlete, overall. Athletes are usually not worried about anything else in high school other than working hard enough in their sport to receive a scholarship. They sometimes tend to put aside everything else that plays a key role and mainly shift their focus onto their sport and receiving a scholarship.

During my recruiting process, I ended up taking only one visit and making my decision shortly after. Getting the opportunity to get a free education was really what caught my eye during the full process. Growing up, I assumed that my Mom would be the one paying for college or I would have to get student loans if she wasn't able to.

I understood at an early age that college was not free and

cost a significant amount of money. Imagine raising four girls on your own and having to then worry about paying for all four tuitions in the future by yourself. I knew it was going to be a lot of stress on her, so I was more than grateful that I could receive such a blessing.

Looking back, I know I made the decision too quickly without checking into my other options due to fear of running out of time and possibly ending up where I did not want to be. When I say "fear", I am referring to the fear of pressure to decide. I was discovered late because I was not exposed to the AAU world until the summer before my senior season and the high school I played at was not well known at the time.

Recruiting for me started later than average. The timeframe seemed short, making it impossible to seriously consider every school that was recruiting me.

When you are in high school, you are maybe 18 or younger making decisions that will affect you for the rest of your life and career. The recruiting process can be overly exciting, but it can also be incredibly stressful, exhausting, and sometimes a lengthy process for some. The pressure comes from different avenues whether it is college coaches implicitly pressuring you to decide on them or your parents anxious for you to finally pick a school and get rid of the constant calls, mails, and visits.

There is a difference between college coaches showing interest and contacting you versus having a lot of college coaches offering you scholarships. The expectations are quite different and the level of stress on an athlete depends on which part of the process they are at.

When coaches are simply interested, all they want to do is get to know you and figure out what type of athlete and kid you are. Most of the time, they already know what type of an athlete you are from watching your games throughout the summer and school year. All they are interested in now is getting to know you on a personal level. At this stage, the athlete is more relaxed mentally, but is still not complacent because the coach can withdraw their interest at any given moment.

However, when an athlete has been offered a full athletic scholarship by multiple schools, some coaches and athletic programs tend to pressure the athletes into a decision even when they know the athlete has other options to consider. Most coaches believe that if the athlete is good enough for them, the athlete must make the decision to commit right away if the scholarship is offered. Most athletic programs do not understand that they also must be a good fit for the athlete, who must weigh both their education and athletic responsibilities when making these decisions.

Often, coaches will try to force an expiration date. They plant the seed in the athlete's mind to rush their decision before their offer is withdrawn and given to another athlete that is next in line. At this point, athletes who are considering multiple scholarships fear not being able to find something better down the line, so they sign their letter of intent to a program or university that they think is a good fit and drop their other options.

The coach I signed my letter of intent under was a great coach and an even better person. I got the opportunity not only to explore the school and the athletic department, but also to visit and have multiple conversations with the head coach and her assistants. At the time, I had other great coaches and universities recruiting me.

I could have waited it out and have gone somewhere better

than where I ended up program wise. However, the relationship I established initially and automatically with the coach and her staff attracted me to the school and played a huge role in my commitment to that university and athletic program.

I knew the program I was coming into was not particularly good, but I believed in the coach's vision for the program as well as her vision for me. She was already making an impact at the school, so I wanted to be a part of a success journey and build my own legacy alongside her and the program.

Unfortunately, things didn't go as planned. When the coach got an opportunity somewhere else, I, as an incoming freshman was still forced to attend that school and play under the new coach who replaced her. I was informed that according to NCAA rules, unless the coach coming in releases me from the scholarship I signed under, I was not able to leave and go elsewhere.

During this time, I was upset and thought it was unfair and unjust that coaches can leave whenever they can without penalty, but athletes cannot do the same and have a lot more consequences. I felt I was recruited into a situation and then left to figure it out all on my own with a completely new coaching staff that I didn't even know or sign under.

If the coach the athlete signs under either gets an opportunity elsewhere or unfortunately gets fired, the athlete should have the opportunity to find happiness somewhere else that is more fitting or comfortable. The problematic thing that can backfire on the athlete is if the coach leaves just before the athlete's first year and there aren't a lot of scholarship options due to availability and timing around that short time period. Nine times out of ten, coaches and athletic programs have their desired athletes ramping up to the school year.

Decommitting from a school late in the game is risky and can place the athlete in situations where there is no wiggle room or good options. It is still important that the athlete be given the choice and option to either stay and play for the new coach and the staff or leave and find a program that would be more fitting for them. Often when athletes commit, they do not necessarily commit to universities for their educational opportunities, they commit to athletic programs and their coaches for athletic reasons.

So, if a coach leaves or unfortunately gets fired, often the athlete now becomes uncomfortable with being placed under someone else that is not familiar with their playing style or personality. That is where relationships between coaches and athletes sometimes go downhill and transferring is brought to the mix the following year. The athlete is not thinking, "This is a good school academically, I should stay." The athlete is thinking, "My coach left. I do not want to stay here and play under a stranger that does not know my playing style."

This is not to say that I was necessarily "forced" into the decision I made nor am I saying I regret signing under who I initially signed my letter of intent with. This is to say that we as athletes during the recruiting stage of the process often get pressured into deciding because we are not only fighting time, but we are also competing with other recruits that currently might also be getting recruited by the same college coaches themselves.

I would like to compare recruiting to dating for a second. When coaches show interest, you are dating them, and they are dating you. They will check in here and there and might even attend some of your games. They will call you and try to get to know you. They also might text you or your high school coaches to try and get more information on you.

They want to know your likes and dislikes and figure out what type of personality you have. When they are expressing interest, it just means that they like you and they might want to eventually make you an offer, but they have other options as well that they might be considering.

Sometimes you may be a priority on the list, or you could be just another athlete they have interest in but aren't ready to take the next steps with at that time.

When you are dealing with coaches that have interest, you feel a little bit more at ease and you can take your time and not stress about deciding. The most important part of this stage to remember is, both sides can withdraw their interest at any point during this stage if compatibility is not there. There is no commitment tying both parties down.

On the other hand, when you have been offered a scholarship, it is different. This represents when someone you have gone on some dates with expresses their feelings towards you and is wanting you to do the same and hopefully get a committed relationship out of it. The problem is, if you are dating a lot of athletic programs and a few express their feelings and offer you scholarships, the process then becomes a little stressful. Deciding becomes a burden instead of a positive and fun experience.

Schools will consistently contact you to see where you are at with your options and if they feel they are not a top priority on your list, they might withdraw their scholarships or consider other options to protect themselves in case you do not consider them as a choice in the future. The reason is, colleges must fill up their rosters too. They have a certain number of athletes they must recruit, not just for the current year, but years to come. They plan ahead. If they feel an athlete is not interested enough, they will start looking   so they are not left to settle with athletes they never intended to make a commitment to.

Although this issue is prevalent with some universities and colleges, there are some colleges and universities that are faithful to the athlete and will stay in the game, stick by their side through the process, and hope that they are the school that best fits their educational and athletic needs.

I saw this video on social media that depicted a kid with four or five options during national signing day. He chose a school that he thought best fit his needs and wants, but his parent did not think so. The most disheartening and uncomfortable part of that video was the reaction of the parent when the athlete chose a school that was different than what the parent had in mind.

As a parent, you know what is best for your kid because you are the one that raised them. When it comes to these situations, it is best that you still support but let them make their own decisions. There is nothing wrong with offering your opinions as most athletes need it but supporting your athlete no matter the school they choose to study and compete at is the greatest feeling ever.

I made my decision because of the coach and the plan for the program as well as the plans for me individually as a player and person. I wanted to be a part of the rebuilding of a program, make history and reap the benefits as success came. I also knew I wanted to be close to home.

At the time, although education played a significant role in where I attended college, I was honestly only focused on choosing a school that fit my idea of what kind of coach and program I wanted to play for. Every decision that was made about this process was coming from the athletic aspect of it. And because of this, as athletes, we put ourselves in predicaments of only valuing a school based on the success of their athletic program and not considering their academic program.

Going into college, my expectations were of those you might see in movies. Do you remember that 2000 movie called "Love and Basketball"? Yes? Well, that's how I thought college was going to be for me. Sad to say, I quickly found out otherwise. There was no "love and basketball", just basketball and unfortunately, love (in the movie, Quincy) was nowhere to be found either.

Academically, college was not that hard for me. I loved school, learning, and making good grades. I was also a competitive person, so I was determined to get the highest GPA on the team. Winning awards because of my GPA gave me a sense of accomplishment. I valued education and I always considered my life outside of my sport. I also took myself out of that athletic role often to identify and test myself to see if I had a professional career I would be interested in pursuing, if I was not successful in the professional sport life.

I've always thought backup plans were healthy and good for people to think about and consider, because you never know what could happen to you physically as an athlete. Our sports are tough and require a lot of us physically as well as mentally. I always thought well, if I were to get a second injury towards the end of the season and my chances at the professional life were delayed, did I have a backup plan for me to transition into after graduation.

It is vital that athletes should often think beyond their sport. Although sports are both mental and physical, you rely more on your physical attributes to carry you through your sport career life. When those physical attributes start shutting down or something terrible happens to us physically, what are we to do next? Those are the types of questions athletes should be asking themselves. As a coach mentoring and looking after these athletes for four, five years, I think it is necessary to ask your athletes these questions and pick their brains to see how they are thinking.

In retrospect, I would have been more prepared if I knew what kind of world I was stepping into. I honestly feel like I could have had a much better career and would have made better decisions in terms of my professional life if I were more knowledgeable about the process then. Throughout my college career, I had multiple coaching changes, injuries, and other issues that were hard to experience at that age regarding my sport. Even though there were some struggles throughout my career, I made it through and had the opportunity to continue my career playing professionally in Europe.

Although it was a journey, I believe it was a journey that God designed for me to walk, and my experiences inspired me to, in return, inspire the youth and inform them on important topics that I know most are not aware of.

Most athletes and their coaches and parents are so clueless and blind to this world in which their athletes are living. When I was getting recruited before college, my Mom was not involved. It was not because she did not care about me, but because she was uninformed and uneducated about the topic. She did not know what to communicate or how to communicate with the coaches.

She wanted to be involved, but she did not know how. Most

of her concern was obtaining the scholarship and getting a degree in the end. She did not know what she needed to do to prepare me for college athletics. I took on everything myself. I tried making these life-changing decisions by myself at the age of 17 to the best of my abilities.

Just as we have good coaches in this world that do right by the athlete, we also have ones that are not honest and truthful with their athletes. Certain coaches will sell you a dream to get you to commit to their school. If coaches were honest and real with their recruits and college athletes, the trust aspect of the relationship would naturally appear, and players would be willing and ready to do any and everything for their coaches. Unfortunately, college athletics is a business. Just like sales in the business world, college coaches compete against other schools make their programs   sound and look appealing so that they catch the attention of the best athletes.

Throughout and after my college career, I've witnessed players, current players, and even ex-players' lives affected by this. Some athletes end up developing mental issues regarding such matters. Athletes are not being properly taken care of, and they are also not taking care of themselves, as they should when they are in college. When an athlete commits his or her life to sports, that's all they have. If sports are not going well for them, they tend to believe that their entire world is crashing down. Everything in their lives is viewed in a negative light because they are not excelling in their sport.

The solution to this is not only for coaches to check in on their players, but for them to be able to help athletes cope better with problems they might be experiencing within their sport, to help them find solutions, and know that they have purpose beyond their sport.

The reason why I understand and connect well is because I

was and still am an athlete myself. I went through the very things I mentioned, and I was a strong enough person to get through them and come out mentally tougher than I was going in. Due to my experience and other athletes' experiences, I was extremely passionate and eager to attack such issues that are misunderstood and misconceived by high school athletes everywhere, the public, and their support systems helping athletes make these life changing decisions.

I wanted to share information and help student athletes make better decisions with regard to choosing colleges, taking their education seriously, and understanding and accepting the transitional period after their sport. I have learned that it is better to be informed, take precautions, and put your best foot forward going into a situation than not being aware or prepared and struggling the whole way through and having regrets after. My hope is to help someone that might be clueless about this process or is already in college for one year and is trying to figure everything out on their own.

You are most definitely valued beyond your sport and should value yourselves as well. You are more than your athletic identity and the sooner you understand that, the better life after retirement will be. Take your education seriously and have fun with your sport. Although it comes with a lot of demands, time requirements, and stress sometimes, it is a great learning opportunity that will teach you a lot and give you many memories. Positive or negative, being a college athlete changes your life.

CHAPTER 2

Is it what it seems to be

Perception is the way we interpret or understand something through our own experiences and ideas. It is the process of thought before experiencing the situation and finding out the reality of it. Our perception is what we think something is like or will be like. Everybody has their own perception, but our perceptions are shaped by what we see, hear, and ultimately what we are told. Before entering a situation in which we have never previously been, we seek advice from those that either have been in those situations themselves or have information due to their connections. Sometimes we get information from the source themselves and other times we get it from a third party, which means we got it from someone that got it from somebody else.

Going into college, most of us have a certain perception. But having a perception of something sometimes does not always prepare us for the reality of that situation that is to come later. As young athletes with dreams of playing at the college level, we might have perceptions of how college is going to be, but what we fail to consider is all aspects of college athletics and not just the sport.

College for us is not just academics and it is not just athletics, it is both. I had the pleasure of interviewing a few athletes from different sports and conferences to speak on their perceptions of what they thought college athletics was going to be like before they entered that world. Although they are from different sports and athletic programs, the experience of being an athlete is comparable.

TJ Taylor is a University of North Texas Alumni who was a part of the men's basketball team from 2012-2015. Before attending the University of North Texas, TJ went to Denison High school and was recruited to Oklahoma. Unfortunately, he suffered a season-ending injury prior to Oklahoma's 2010-2011 season opener.

"Going into college I didn't know anything, I was a kid. I was blind to everything," he told me. "My perception of it did not turn out to be what it was. My eyes were not open to the fact that it can be a shady business sometimes. The sad thing is, nobody communicates this to us or warns us athletes of it until we are going through it and realize it in the end for ourselves."

Carnae Dillard is a San Antonio native who played volleyball at Lady Bird Johnson High. She went on to compete at the collegiate level at the University of North Texas where she achieved illustrious career success. Carnae was a two-time conference USA player of the year and earned All-American honorable mention honors as a senior. She also finished as the program's leader in attacks and kills in a season. Carnae did not stop there. She got the opportunity to go professional in volleyball, playing overseas in Sweden where she continued her success journey. She was voted player of the year, the highest award in the Elitserien league.

"My perception was that I was going to be the best and I wanted to play the sport I loved and have fun doing it. I feel like in my four years I did just that," she said. "I didn't know it would be the hardest but most rewarding feeling waking up every day at 5:30 a.m., going to weights, then class, then having a 3-4-hour practice, and then tutoring, just to wake up the next day and do it all over again. It was super tough, but so worth it."

Aluk Adub is a South Sudanese athlete from Jacksonville, Florida. Aluk graduated from the Potters House Christian academy in 2011. Prior to his season at University of West Alabama Tigers (UWA), he played two seasons at Florida State college in Jacksonville. At Florida State college, he averaged 14.6 points per game while shooting 53.5 percent from the field and 44.4 percent from the 3-point arc. Aluk is now playing professionally in Europe for an extremely competitive team in Madrid, Spain.

"My perception was that college was going to be ok, not too hard," he said. "I knew I was going to be away from my family a lot when I got to college. I did not know the amount of stress basketball was going to put on me both physically and mentally. I think that stress played a huge roll on why I shifted my focus from both academics and athletics to just athletics, making it easier on me. It wasn't my best decision, but it was the decision I made at the time which I regret fully now."

Taylor Roof graduated from Marcus High school where she maintained a perfect 4.0 throughout her high school career. Taylor earned first team all-district honors and second team District 6-6A pick in her senior year. She was recruited with a scholarship to play basketball at the University of North Texas where her first season was taken from her before it even started. Taylor suffered a season-ending knee injury in practice, forcing her to sit on the sidelines and cheer her teammates on as she dealt with a tough, slow healing injury.

"My perception going into college was definitely pretty spot on," she told me. "I was ready for my freedom and getting to do what I wanted. With freedom comes responsibilities though. I had to learn how to take care of myself on my own and clean up after myself, do laundry, cook for myself, buy myself groceries, gas, and do whatever other upkeep I needed."

"I had to manage my time and keep myself organized with school, basketball, and extracurriculars. Before, I didn't realize all the details that went into college and being on my own. It took me awhile to understand what I needed to do to help myself succeed but once I realized that, college seemed a lot easier as a student athlete."

Austin Mitchell graduated from high school in Plano, Texas, where he averaged 16.3 points per game as a senior at Plano. He was named first-team all-district 8-5A and was ranked 12th among all players in the Dallas-Fort Worth area. Austin passed up offers, thinking he would get better ones and ended up at the University of North Texas where he earned a walk-on scholarship for his 2012-2013 season. Austin then transferred out of the University of North Texas, went to Hesston College, and then finally ended up at Bethel College where he decided to retire from basketball. He is now a motivational speaker empowering the youth.

"I thought college was going to be all fun and some school work," he said. "I didn't realize how many opportunities college had within athletics and outside of athletics. I had no idea it was so diverse and that I was going to meet the amount of people that I did. I also did not know how much athletes were valued on campus due to their athletic status."

Alexis Hyder graduated from LBJ high school in Austin, Texas. She got a scholarship to compete at the University of North Texas before transferring out and entering the Southeastern Conference (SEC) with the Louisiana State University (LSU) Tigers. She was named Louisiana Sports

Writers Association (LSWA) newcomer of the year, made the All-Louisiana second team, earned honorable mention Associated Press All-SEC and received the offensive player of the year award on her LSU women's basketball team. Hyder is now in her second season as a professional basketball player in Sweden.

"My perception was different than that of what I went through all of my college career," she says. "Looking back now, I wish I knew the power of connections. My school provided plenty of job fair opportunities and motivating seminars for both women and athletes. But when you are in college, you don't see the value in those resources until later. "

"No one is there looking over your back, making sure you attend those things because that is a responsibility of your own which you should take seriously. It almost feels like a chore, instead of something beneficial to you or your career, overall. At some athletic programs, the help is there, you just have to request it. If you don't recognize the help, you must ask for it. You should not be afraid of needing help in any situation."

Hearing these life stories, you come to understand that perceptions are not helpful if they are not realistic. You can imagine something to be like what you've seen in the past, what you've heard from other people, or even from what you've been told, but until you experience it yourself, you wouldn't truly know what it's like.

For example, before going to college, I viewed college through the media lens and how it was mainly exposed to me through T.V., as silly as that sounds. I thought college was like love and basketball or other movies and shows I've seen that portrayed college in a certain way. Just because we have a predetermined idea of how something is supposed to be or is going to be, does not mean those initial perceptions are true. Usually when you want advice on something you've never done before, you would go to someone that is knowledgeable about the subject who can help steer you in the right direction.

There is nothing out there in the world that can prepare you one-hundred percent for something that has not yet happened to you and set you up for guaranteed success. However, there are tools that can help prepare and guide you in the right direction so that you are aware and know your options if the situations were to come up during your journey. Consider this book a tool you can use to help guide you through your journey.

CHAPTER 3

Recruitment

Preparing for college athletics means understanding your chances of receiving a scholarship and understanding the recruiting process and its flow. After high school, not every athlete is able to continue playing his or her sport at the next level due to little or no recruitment which is based on talent level and sometimes grades. For those that get that chance, whether you have 20 or 200 schools looking to recruit you, do your due diligence and choose a school based on your educational needs first and athletic needs second. Realize that your sport will one day end (for many reasons) and your degree will lead you into your next path in life.

Also, most universities do not offer certain degree opportunities and educational opportunities like others do. If you choose a school based on athletics, and you graduate with a degree that has no purpose for you, it may be tough trying to find a job in the degree you chose to pursue in college. It is already tough for non-athletic students to obtain career jobs after college. Imagine a student athlete who did not get internship opportunities or job opportunities in college to help build their resumes along the way.

According to the National Collegiate Athletics Association (NCAA), only about 2% of high school athletes earn an athletic scholarship to college. NCAA division I and division II schools provide more than $2.9 billion in athletic scholarships annually to student athletes. Division III schools do not offer athletic aid and might receive their funding from other parts of the university but not from the athletic department itself. Typically, full scholarships cover tuition and fees, room, board, and course related books for classes. Not all athletes receive full scholarships. In fact, most athletes who receive athletic aid receive an amount to cover a portion of the cost and then financial aid or academic scholarships take care of the other portion if the athlete is eligible.

After you understand your chances of receiving a scholarship, next comes the recruitment process and dealing with coaches and athletic programs. Most parents understand their athlete has a scholarship, but they do not understand the totality of it and the process that the athlete goes through. Usually, the role of the parent during this time is to mentor and guide the athlete through a successful, less stressful recruitment process. It is also to help the athlete notice any red flags that might indicate a university or college might not be the right fit for the athlete.

It is important that parents communicate with college coaches and try to establish a relationship, so the athlete becomes comfortable and trusting of the coach. If I were a parent, I would want to know exactly who the coach is and what kind of school I would possibly be sending my kid to for the next four years of his or her life. Most people do not consider it so, but those four to five years in college matter to the athlete and will be cherished and remembered for the rest of their lives.

Those pivotal years spark a journey and transition into adulthood. I do not believe most coaches are aware of this. Coaches have so much control and a great amount of access to the athlete during those years. Good or bad, they have influence and power over the athletes competing for them. They have control over their time, and for some athletes, control over their mental state and confidence level. The sad truth is, there are more coaches that do not care for athletes and their well-being than there are good coaches that care for the athlete apart from their sport.

I have come to understand and realize that, college athletics is a big business and if the student athlete performs a certain way, they do not care what the student athlete does outside of their sport. They care about numbers and success within the sport and the university . They care about generating fans, money, and wealth towards the athletic department and the school. What people do not think about is, what is the athlete getting out of this? How is the athlete benefiting from all this success the school is receiving apart from a free education?

Let's think and reflect on the NCAA tournament for a second. Each year, athletes sacrifice and train all year to win their regular season and conference games so that they might have the possibility of making the NCAA tournament to fight for a championship. There is both stress on the university, coach, and the athlete to compete well and win. But at the end of the day, the athlete is the one directly affected.

They are the ones competing in the tournament day in and day out and the ones who end up not earning a single thing other than some T-shirts, hats, and perhaps the NCAA championship ring. Of course, earning a national championship is great and every athlete aspires to do so. But at the end of it all, the university, athletic program, and the coach are the ones that truly benefit.

When the athlete is done, can that university and athletic program say they did all they could have done to make sure the athlete had all the tools to succeed in life beyond their sport?

Yes, some athletes do make it professionally and do not have to use their degree right away, but what about the ones who don't get the opportunity? Would you say they were well off and prepared for the next phase in their lives?

I believe in accountability and discipline, and athletes should possess those characteristics, but the NCAA, athletic department, and college coaches can always do more than they do for athletes in the education and life beyond their sports. The university itself can only offer the classes and labs that the athletes need to take, but it's usually up to the athletic department to guide, mentor, and aid the student athlete towards a path they will be successful in.

I had an opportunity to interview more athletes on both their past and current college athletic experiences:

Norrisha Victrum graduated from Columbia High school where she was recognized as one of the top-five female basketball players in the state of South Carolina for the 2011-12 season. After high school, she went on to play point guard for "Thundering Herd" at Marshall University, where she led the team in various categories including assists, steals, and minutes per game.

"I do not think that coaches and athletic programs prepare kids for life after sports because some simply do not care," she said. "Nine times out of ten, the kids will not keep in touch with their coaches after they graduate or even come back to visit their college athletic programs. Coaches and athletic departments are only concerned with the player when they are competing for their programs. When the athlete's eligibility is over, they have no use or benefit from them anymore so that's when they part ways and the relationship is lost before it was ever established."

Norrisha's viewpoint is similar to my own. Although coaches do sometimes tell you what you want to hear instead of what you need to hear, you ultimately make the decision in the end. It is impossible to put all the blame on the coaches without the athlete also taking responsibility. Yes, coaches do say certain things that might appeal more to you than others to sell their school, but at the end of the day, you are the one choosing that city, that degree, that program, that coach, that team, that university.

As a recruit, you have the opportunity during the process to go on an "official" or "unofficial" visit to visit the coaching staff, the team, and the university itself. During this process, you should have a list of questions in mind of what you are looking for academically and athletically to help determine during that visit if that school you are visiting would be a good fit for you.

It is wise to never decide based on the athletic program alone because some colleges specialize in certain degrees. This is something to consider, especially if the school is appropriate for you athletically but not academically.

An athletic scholarship to study the degree of your choice is not just a blessing, but it is a fantastic opportunity to seek and study something else other than your sport. Be confident in your judgment, make wise decisions and always seek help for other opinions. If your parents are not involved for whatever reason, whether it is because they are not informed or aware of the process or they are just not interested in that part of the process, talk to your coaches or friends.

I also recommend that you reach out to an athlete that may still be in college or maybe an athlete that already graduated. Seek advice and pick their brains on things you might not understand or might be unsure of. Do your research to be sure you fit that system and university before committing.

How you experience this will depend on you at that point. I understand you cannot control everything, but you can always control how you react and deal with situations. Select a school that values you as more than an athlete and that cares to invest in you and your future, whether it is the professional athletic world or the professional work world after graduation.

Candice Followwell graduated from Sachse High School and went on to play college basketball at the University of Arkansas Fort Smith. She led the team in assists, earned an award as conference player of the week, was third on the team in scoring and second on the team for rebounds. Candice is now an assistant women's basketball coach for the Coffeyville red ravens.

"First, let's start with the fact that up until 10th grade I was split on playing soccer or basketball in college," she said. "Once I made the decision for basketball, I started AAU. Since I started AAU so late and I wasn't the tallest player, I didn't stand out as much to schools I thought/knew I could play for. Out of high school, I was originally committed to a Division III but decommitted due to financial decisions I had to make for my own good and future. I made 4 visits total and had extraordinarily little college coach contact. I had one full ride offer, and other small offers. I went to the school that believed in me and that offered me the money they thought I was worth. Recruiting for me wasn't this huge deal, but I also turned my back on junior colleges, which would have been a great option for me due to the lack of exposure I had."

Nekia Jones graduated from Ozen High School in Beaumont, TX, where she was ranked as the number 58th overall recruit in the class of 2013 according to ESPN news reports. Winning various awards both in basketball and track, Nekia got recruited to play basketball at the University of Texas where she played 2 years before transferring out and attending the University of North Texas. Nekia then left the University of North Texas and joined the Ragin' Cajuns, where she finished her playing career.

"I think college coaches need to be real with themselves before recruiting kids in to their schools" she said. "It's best that they mention the good and the bad that comes with being a student athlete. This is so that the athlete knows ahead of time what to expect and not have to wonder and be thrown into the situation their first year and don't have the ability to deal or cope effectively. When I was getting recruited in middle school and high school, I would get so many calls throughout the day. Looking back, it was a lot for someone of my age to deal with and make life changing decisions. I was glad that I had parents that were involved and helped me through the process, I think it definitely helped me a lot."

Now a professional basketball player, Norrisha Victrum said, "I do not think that coaches are honest with their recruits. I think every coach tells their recruits what they want to hear instead of what they need to hear. Some coaches even reach the point of telling their players that they will automatically play and disregard the fact that not every athlete at that level will have the opportunity to earn the same amount of playing time due to several reasons. Playing time isn't automatically given, it is earned, and it is earned when you get there not before no matter how "good" you are coming out of high school."

"When these athletes finally get to college, they expect to play or start due to what was communicated to them by the coaches and when that doesn't happen, they start to lose confidence in themselves and consider solutions such as transferring. Most of the time, it is even tougher for those athletes that come from being an "All-Star" on their high school teams to not even touching the court at all on game days."

"College coaches are a little deceiving when recruiting but mostly your performance is what makes the situation different. Coaches have an idea in their mind of what type of player you are and how you can help their program. But if you come to college and become a slacker, they are less inclined to be as nice as they were during the recruiting process. Athletes must keep in mind that it's a business and coaches' jobs are on the line. As an athlete, we are looking for a family because we were basically kids when entering college but having your own support system back home is more important than the people you are around in college" said former LSU alumni Alexis Hyder.

Ashley Henry is a track star who graduated from Liberty High School in Frisco, Texas, and got a scholarship to the University of North Texas for the 2012-13 season before transferring out and attending the University of Georgia. Ashley competed in the 55-meter dash, 60-meter dash, 100-meter dash, 200-meter dash and ran the 4X100 relay as well as the 4X400 meter relay in which she competed well and earned awards.

"I don't believe college coaches are honest with their recruits during the recruiting process," she said. "They paint this grand picture for the athlete and leave out the reality of it all. When I was in college and we had recruits come on their visits, I was always chosen as a host and I believe I too was involved in painting that picture for the athlete as well. I think when an athlete finally commits to a school, it is all about coping mechanisms as nothing is really like what it seems in the beginning after that point."

"It gets real after that recruiting stage and every decision you make past that point is on you. A question I would ask is, can you make the best out of your situation you weren't properly prepared for? This happened to me when I was competing in college. The first university I attended, the coaching staff within that program were insensitive. When I transferred out, I faced more challenges with my next school than I thought I would. At my new school, I felt secluded from the entire population because I was an athlete who happened to be African American. It was definitely a culture shock to experience such a thing at the college level and it made me realize a lot."

Hearing from these athletes, it is evident that Selecting the best program for you is not only important but essential for one's future success. You must be within the right system to achieve the type of success you are looking for. Do not be afraid to ask questions that will give you insight into what kind of coach, program, and university you might be playing for.

"I've known and have seen talented players that do not play much due to the type of players they are playing with on the roster. A lot of athletes get so caught up in the name of the school that they lose other aspects of the process and don't consider how their decisions will impact them individually going forward.

The problem sometimes is not that they are not talented, but that their team is full of talented players so now it's who can do what better. Athletes need to be prepared to ask coaches tough questions and pick their minds on what they see the future looking like with them on the roster. Obviously, there isn't a definite yes or no question because nobody can really foresee the future, but they can give a glimpse of maybe what it might look like with them in the lineup.

Athletes need to also take ownership of their careers and not rely on others to hold their lives in their hands. They are your coaches and they are there for your support, but you are still accountable for you and everything you want to accomplish as well as what type of legacy you want to leave behind", said Karen Blair.

Karen Blair is the women's basketball assistant coach at the University of Maryland. Karen suggests the following sample questions that you might consider asking coaches recruiting you:

1. What is the culture of your team?

2. What is your coaching style and at what pace do you like to play?

3. What is your current need on the team right now?

4. How do I fit into your system?

5. Are there any other positions that you see me possibly playing?

6. What are the strengths and weaknesses of the team currently?

7. What is a typical schedule for the team?

8. What can I do to prepare myself for this role and college athletics?

9. Regarding the number of recruits, you are presently

THE REALITY BEHIND THE GLAMOUR OF COLLEGE ATHLETICS

recruiting in my current position, where do I rank?

10. You've seen me play throughout the summer, what do you think I can improve or work on prior to college?

11. What is the team's GPA and what do athletes at that school typically major in?

12. Do you provide this major I am looking to get a degree in?

13. I am aware that as a freshman, I will not automatically get playing time, but what would I need to do to earn playing time?

14. Does the athletic program provide workshops that will help with my future professional career?

15. What do you look for in a leader?

16. I have professional aspirations in my sport. Do you think you will be able to help me, to the best of your abilities, reach my goal?

As Karen suggests, these are just sample questions, but these questions help the coach understand what your expectations are and what you are looking for in a university or college to see if you fit their system. Just as you want to see if their system fits your needs, they want to see if you fit their system and aspirations for the program going forward.

CHAPTER 4

Financial aid vs. athletic aid

Financial aid is any form of aid that is provided to students to pay for college if not given the opportunity to obtain a full scholarship that covers tuition, books, and room and board. There are several types of financial aid, including federal loans, state grants, financial aid, and academic aid. As athletes, we can receive full or partial athletic scholarships to pay for school but not every athlete gets that opportunity and not every school is able to provide those scholarships equally.

An athletic scholarship is an amount of financial aid awarded to a student athlete from their athletic department. Athletic aid does not come from other areas of the school and is supported solely by the athletic department. How they internally get that money and support can depend on numerous factors such as boosters, ticket sales, away games, donations, and media coverages.

Statistically speaking, there is a significantly small number of athletes that are blessed enough to receive athletic scholarships immediately after high school and an even smaller number of athletes that receive athletic aid at the division I level. While division I and II schools get their aid from the athletic department to provide full or partial scholarships, division III schools and the ivy leagues look for aid within other areas of school than the athletic department. Ivy league and division III schools do not and cannot offer athletic scholarship aid to their student athletes. Only division I schools within certain sports can guarantee full rides, and the other sports are considered what they call "equivalency" sports.

This means that the NCAA determines how much money a program or university can invest and spend on a sport such as track. That is why some athletes on a track team might have partial scholarships while very few have full scholarships. According to the NCAA rules and regulations, it is up to the coaches as to how and to whom they offer the athletic scholarships.

There are six recognized sports that automatically get the opportunity to give full athletic aid to their student athletes from division I schools. These sports include football, women's and men's basketball, tennis, volleyball, and gymnastics. In these sports at the division I level, you either receive full aid or no aid.

Full athletic aid to a student athlete depends on the athlete's athletic ability within their sport, the availability of scholarships to offer for the program, and the potential and impact that player might make if presented with the scholarship. Division II schools can offer scholarships, but often can't offer free education. Junior colleges are a different story. They have their own national junior college athletics association that awards full or partial scholarships to compete at that level.

Athletes can be confused into thinking that if a coach verbally offers a scholarship, it is definite, and they will end up at that university or college. My advice is to be extremely cautious and careful with those verbal commitments.

I have heard stories from athletes in which they were verbally offered a scholarship. When it was time to collect, the coach found another athlete that better suited him that he wanted to offer the scholarship to, but it was never communicated by the coach. If the scholarship is not offered in writing, you are not yet awarded that scholarship and are still competing with other prospects being considering for that same scholarship.

Most people do not realize it, but athletic aid is incredibly competitive. You can be an extremely good athlete, but if that school does not have the athletic aid to offer you, chances are you won't have a scholarship. That is why education is imperative regardless of your athletic ability because athletes can also receive academic scholarships if they meet the criteria and requirements of that institute.

Whenever they choose to, coaches can change their minds on a prospect and withdraw their verbal commitments. Athletic aids are also yearly based and not technically a four-year commitment even though it seems that way. This means that if you received an athletic scholarship to a division I school, at the end of every year, you sign to renew your scholarship for the next year.

Though it is sad that there aren't enough full scholarships to go around, there are other options athletes have to pay for their education. Aside from academic aid which depends on grades, students can fill out an online application through Free Application for Federal Student Aid (FAFSA) to determine their financial aid eligibility within their university or college institution.

They must complete this application before college for student athletes entering college, and after every academic year to ensure that the application gets reviewed in a timely manner. If you are unfamiliar with FAFSA and need more information, it is best that you talk to your high school counselor. For those already in college, talk with your college coaches, teammates, and the financial aid center located on campus.

Some aid from FAFSA can be free, while other aid you may need to pay back upon graduation. These are called loans. Even though financial aid might be provided to some athletes in forms of grants and loans, some athletes do not get that opportunity to receive grants.

To qualify for grants (money you do not have to pay back) through FAFSA, there are certain requirements and criteria you must meet to be eligible for grant aid. One of the biggest requirements by the government is household income. If your parents make over a certain amount of money, you as the athlete will not have the opportunity to receive grant aid while in college. The reason is grants usually work on a certain family contribution basis. So, if your family makes a certain amount of money over the limit they consider to be the median, you will most likely not receive a grant.

Most of the time, student athletes in high school are clueless of the fact that just being offered a scholarship does not mean that you are automatically accepted into the school. Since the education aspect of college is neglected and not really thought about, student athletes oftentimes do not know or understand that to attend that school, you would need to apply to that school and take the SAT or the ACT tests, which are required by most colleges for admission purposes. There is no preference where one is valued more than the other but if you have concerns, it does not hurt to call the admissions office of the college you are applying to and ask. Typically, colleges accept either of the two, but it does not ever hurt to ask for assurance. When deciding on which test to take, make sure to consider the differences and look at which one will benefit you in terms of performance and scores as it is critical for admission chances. For accurate test dates and more information, visit the College Board website and browse through the page for information related to your questions and concerns.

Typically speaking, it costs money to take the SAT and ACT tests, but these waivers are intended to help students so that they do not have to pay the first few times. Be sure to also ask either your high school coaches or counselors for test waivers.

If you are eligible for this waiver, you will be able to receive a maximum of two waivers which you can use to take the test free of charge. You have the option to get the wavier your junior year or senior year, but the waiver does expire on a certain date. Plan accordingly and try to take the test earlier rather than later in case you may need to attempt it again. Do not wait until the last minute to take the test and then give yourself no chance at another attempt. If you have made the decision that you will compete in college athletics and go to college, start thinking about these things at least at the beginning of your junior year.

There are also tools and books available that can help you prepare and study for this test so that you are able to understand the test and the material that you will be required to know. The book, which I myself got my junior year, contains sample questions and directions on how to take the test as well as how to understand the test. In addition to taking the SAT or ACT, you are also required to submit your transcript along with an essay to the university's admissions office for their review. Most of the time, they will send you a topic for the essay. When drafting this essay, seek help from your coaches, parents, or elders who are a part of your support system. Have them help you with this process so it turns out as smoothly as possible.

It is imperative, especially in your junior year, to create a to-do list and check off items as you complete them. You should always keep your grades up, talk with your counselor frequently, and try to be prepared academically for the ACT/SAT by the spring. Remember to always do your research and be ahead of the game. The sooner you complete your to-do list and check it off as you go, the easier the process and the better your chances of attending and competing in college, as you planned.

CHAPTER 5

Academics

Pursuing a major of your choice in college is especially important and vital for future professional success. This degree that you work so hard for will provide you with an opportunity to acquire a job in the field in which you graduate. It does not automatically provide you the job, but it gives you more of an opportunity than someone that didn't have the same opportunity to complete a college education.

I believe with a degree, you also need to make connections and create relationships in college so that you multiply your job career opportunities after graduation. For some, that might be right after graduation and for others it might take months to get into your career job. Not everybody ends up working in their field or using their degrees at all and most times end up going back to school to further their education in their desired degrees or discover other skill sets that get them into a different career.

Although there are other factors that go into landing your career job, you should always put yourself in a position to be prepared for that opportunity when it presents itself.

I believe some athletes choose majors that do not pertain to their future professions because some degrees are easier to acquire than others. Some of the reasons some athletes pick "easier" degrees include academic advisors, graduation, time constraints due to their sport, and uncertainty of their career path entering college. It is not true for all, but for some, "athlete" comes first, and "student" comes second. The sad truth is, the sport is taken more seriously. Although athletes need to be disciplined and accountable for themselves, I think the NCAA and some coaches are not doing enough to ensure the success of the student long after graduation. They put importance on "graduating", but what is the goal of graduating if there is no future value or success in the future with that degree? The goal should not be solely to graduate, but to also receive something relevant and meaningful that will long benefit the athlete after their sport. If more athletes spoke out about the importance of education, as they do their own sports, degrees would look a whole lot different.

I had the opportunity to interview Atlanta's ex Women's National Basketball Association (WNBA) and current professional player, Brianna Kiesel. She attended the University of Pittsburgh and graduated in three years in Administration of Justice. Brianna is a proud alum of Pitt and believed her coaches prepared her for life outside of her sport.

"We were provided workshops to attend at Pitt," Brianna said. "They had life skills classes that were mandatory for the athletes to attend. We also had the opportunity to watch our alums come back and tell us what their lives were like and express that transitional period after college. They spoke out about earning those life skills so the transition from your athletic world to your professional world was easier to understand and deal with. The workshops we took taught us how to manage money, draft and edit our resumes as well as interview, and taught us the appropriate etiquette of dining with employers or someone of importance."

She stated that some schools do a respectable job of looking after their athletes, but some do not, which in fact is true. It's usually the bigger conferences such as Atlantic Coast

Conference (ACC), Southeastern Conference (SEC), BIG 12, and American Athletic Conference (AAC), that have more opportunities than lower or mid-major conference schools to provide kids with the resources they need. For athletes to view their education in a different light, the NCAA, and their athletic programs as well as coaches, need to put more value on education as they do athletics.

In October of 2012, there was a tweet made by an athlete named Cardale Jones who attended Ohio State University. His tweet not only made him famous, but also shocked a lot of people considering he was a student-athlete and should have "known better." The tweet read, "Why should we have to go to class if we came here to play FOOTBALL, we ain't come to play SCHOOL, classes are POINTLESS." This is the mind of an athlete who thinks going to college on an athletic scholarship is solely for their sport and that the education aspect is there to keep them playing.

Athletes who think athletics is their sole purpose in college are very mislead and will one day regret their decisions to skip out on their education. What an uncomfortable and embarrassing time the Ohio State athletic department and football team were going through during this time. I wondered how it impacted their university with the entire world judging not only the athlete, but the people in charge of that program. With all the backlash and negative comments that surrounded this situation, did people pause to consider whether there was some truth to his tweet, or did they just assume it was something he had no business expressing to the public at all? Although the athlete got a lot of backlash, I think it was great that he tweeted it at the time he did to bring awareness to the reality of college academics for athletes.

Just like him, most athletes perceive college to be the same way. They don't express this sentiment publicly because it does not only ruin the reputation of the athlete but of the athletic department as well. Instead of taking a deeper look at the situation, people were more concerned with him tweeting the comment than why he tweeted it. They did not ask why most athletes think like this, but instead why an athlete at that level would tweet something of such impact to the world. Many athletes are known for putting a lot of work, time, and energy into their sport, but when it comes to education and their degrees, shy away and put it on the back burner.

I've been around a lot of athletes to be able to tell who cares about their education and who doesn't. For the most part, it is always the people who genuinely value education and people who know they won't have the opportunity at the next level who pursue their degrees as aggressively as they do their sport.

Throughout the years, there have been some academic scandals from well-known schools such as North Carolina, Florida State, and Harvard, to say the very least. The scandals involve academic fraud done to ensure the athlete focuses on their sport more. I believe these scandals happen at every level of competition in college athletics but because high major schools are under a bigger media microscope, they tend to get exposed more and get more heat for their inappropriate and unjust behaviors.

Many athletes might have looked at Cardale's tweet and agreed with his statement about school and classes or even thought it was funny, but what they need to understand is that all it is doing is lessening their potential to be educated and achieve greatness in other things besides their sports. If athletes realized that their sport won't be forever and not everyone gets the same opportunity at the next level, reality would hit for a lot of athletes with misconstrued judgments and perceptions about education.

What happens sometimes is, athletes are placed in easier classes to help boost their GPAs so that they are eligible to play the sport. If the academics do not overshadow or hinder the athlete from performing their sport, it is fine. The fault is not so much on the athlete because they are taught over and over that their sport is important and that if they stay focused and improve their sport skills, they have a chance at the pros.

In most college sports programs, the value of education is nonexistent, which in turn communicates to the athlete that they shouldn't care about academics either. Poor education is one of the many reasons why student athletes continue to fail in life after retirement from their sport. The NCAA appears to be concerned, but are they really? The primary goal for sport programs and NCAA should be to ensure that every athlete gets a quality education that will prepare them for life beyond their sport since they know and typically generate the statistics of playing professionally after college. There are a lot of articles and praise about how a student-athlete does athletically, but rarely do you see anything about academic success. There is nothing that depicts academic achievement of these student athletes that are competing at such an important level athletically.

When I was at the University of North Texas, we had what was called "Mean Green Kickoff". The athletic director at the time, hosted this event to get all the athletes in one room and discuss the previous year's achievements, as well as what to look forward to in the future and set some new goals. At this event, he did not only discuss athletic achievements, but he also discussed academic achievements.

There was this competition each year between teams on which athletic team would get the highest GPA overall and every year it would the same team, but he also recognized people from specific sports that may have not won collectively but had some athletes stand out for their achievements.

As an athlete at the University of North Texas, I was always appreciated for my work in the classroom, as I was appreciated for my work on the court. The fact is, academic success is just as important, or even more important than athletic success. Without an education, your opportunities are limited, and you are not able to reach your full potential and be the best you. When plan A doesn't work, you need a plan B. If you are focused on going to the league, that is fine but make sure you take care of Plan B also which is your education.

The amount of passion, drive, and aggression an athlete puts into the success of his or her sport is amazing. Athletes are resilient, disciplined, and aim for success no matter the obstacles placed in their paths. When your body stops, so does your professional sports career. After that, you must think of other ways to invest in yourself and in your future going forward. Make sure to keep the same energy and put the same effort into your academics as you do your sport.

Aluk Adub reflects, "I did not take my education seriously when I was in school and I took it for granted. I was just there, and it was no problem for me to meet the minimum requirement of passing the class. I was passing, but I did not take in the full opportunity to soak in all the knowledge and wisdom that was given to us in my classes. I regret it because I love learning. I was just too distracted thinking of other things to concentrate and fully understand what it is I was doing and studying."

"I took my education very seriously," said Candice Followwell. "I would like to thank my mother for that. She took the hard road and refused for any of her kids to take the path of lacking a college education. She preached it from the day we could understand what she was saying to us. "Get your education." Education was noticeably big for me, because I had to show her that I was going to be the first Folllowwell to graduate from college.

I always had Plan B, and a Plan C just in case. I wanted to go pro, but if that didn't work, I wanted to coach college basketball, and if that didn't work, I would do something with my major in Marketing. I am currently trying to get my masters in sports management, which will help me towards trying to become a head coach at the collegiate level. I am using my bachelor's degree, but not really using the Marketing aspect of it. "Bachelor's Degree" was all I needed to be able to coach. "Master's Degree" will allow me to be a head coach at the highest level of my choosing."

Taylor Roof said, "I did take my education very seriously because I knew that basketball would not be something I would do for the rest of my life. I am pursuing a degree in Biomedical Engineering and hoping to complete a Master's in Prosthetics and Orthotics. My major was Biomedical Engineering and it still is. I have one year left before earning that degree. I plan to use it to get my master's and make prosthetics and orthotics for individuals who need them."

"I did but I wish I would have really thought through my major I feel like I did the easiest degree and didn't really sit down and figure out what I wanted to do later in life, in better terms I wasn't thinking for the future", said Carnae Dillard. "I knew I wanted to play pro, but I didn't know for how long. After that, coaching was up in the air or being an x-ray tech which I think was a better fit. Kinesiology and not really yes some of the classes helped me but I don't need that specific degree for this field."

Luke Della, "I cared about my education, but I could have taken it more seriously."

Bree McDaniel adds, "I didn't get serious about my grades till my senior year in college. All I was ever worried about growing up was basketball and diverse ways I could grow my game. After I tore my ACL, reality hit, and I had to figure out what I wanted outside of basketball."

Kasiney Williams says, "To a certain extent I knew what I needed to do to continue to play but I could have definitely taken it more serious. My major was integrated studies with a focus in Kinesiology, business, and psychology. I also have two different associate degrees in general studies and in science. I actually work in a pathologist laboratory so in a way I'm using my science degree."

Nekia Jones said, "I didn't really value my education when I was in college. I honestly did enough to get my degree. It wasn't that I was incapable of doing better, it was just me settling and doing the bare minimum to get by. I think a lot of athletes do this which is not helpful to them in the future and they should consider taking their education more seriously than they do nowadays. I think I was given the tools and prepared outside of my sport, but I also made my own adjustments through my college career to try and make it an enjoyable experience for me no matter the circumstances."

Austin Mitchell's outlook is that "I do think education is especially important. Athletes who plan to go pro in their sport a lot of times disregard education just because they believe in themselves. The more time they focus on their sport the better the chance they have at making it pro. Also, unconsciously we as athletes have disregarded education just because a majority of our time is given to athletics and everything that has to do with our sport. Weights, conditioning, practice, games, traveling, film, study hall, etc. I valued my education because I knew I wasn't going to be a pro and wanted a strong resume."

Alexis Hyder reflects, "Unfortunately, I did not invest in my academics as much as I would have liked. However, I believe that was my fault for living the college life and depending on playing professional basketball. My academic advisor persuaded me into my major because it was the majority of my team's degree. I put my trust in her and that was ill advised. I suggest that athletes be involved in the process of their academics."

Norrisha Victrum notes, "I did not take my education as seriously as I should have. My first major was sports medicine, but because I was not as focused in academics, I failed my anatomy class because I wanted to party instead of going to class. The class was during the summer from 8am-12pm. I wanted to enjoy my summer and not be in class. Failing that class ruined my chances of succeeding in my major because I could not take it during the season. So, I ended up changing my major to business administration and worked on sports studies as a minor."

As you have heard, student athletes think that if they put all their energy and focus into their sport in college that they have better chances of making it to the pros than the next athlete. While that is important, your time must be divided up between athletics and your education. It is a balance and one does not have to suffer for the other to thrive.

That's the beauty of what we do and if everybody could do it, everybody would be able to do it. Your abilities are your tools to get you started in life and help you head in the direction you want to go. Do not limit yourself to only one thing and rob yourself of other opportunities presented to you.

In life, opportunities don't come often, and most times do not come without a cost. If you have the chance of going to college, studying a degree of your choice, and playing the sport of your choice, it is only right to satisfy both needs. Never sacrifice one for the other because one depends on the other, but the other doesn't.

Most of the time we are so busy being athletes that we let the student aspect of our lives slip away. For the most part, we do not completely fail because at the end of the day, we need some sort of grades to be able to compete. If the NCAA did not have grade standards for competition, I guarantee you a lot of athletes would not even care about academics all together. They take advantage of the athletic aspect of college but not the student aspect and then are puzzled with life's next plans when they realize that they needed that other aspect as well. When this happens, they are not cheating the school or their coaches nor their teammates. They are only cheating themselves and the endless opportunities they pass up because of their one-track sports mind.

Although coaches and academic advisors play a role, it's also on the student athlete to desire the opportunity for him or herself. If you don't want it yourself, nobody else is going to want it for you. You must be accountable and disciplined within yourself to achieve any type of success in life. Do not choose what is easy to benefit you temporarily. Your sport is temporary.

Do your research on schools, and Select a school that will offer an excellent academic as well as an athletic opportunity. It is termed STUDENT-athlete for a reason, Student first and athlete second. Never make the decision to switch the two.

CHAPTER 6

Competition in college

Athletes today are not like athletes in the past. Hard work isn't valued as much anymore and most depend on their skills to lead them to success in their sports. Honestly speaking, some kids are not suited for college athletics mentally and physically. Coming from high school, you were probably the best player on the team. When you get to college, that is not necessarily the case. You are in a new world, a bigger, more competitive, more athletic, and more skillful world. A mistake that freshman college athletes make is thinking they are better and expecting to be treated like they were in high school. What they do not understand is, to get the praise they want, they must do the work. You do not automatically get praise because you were the best player on your team in high school. At this level, nobody cares about that anymore.

I blame some of this on today's social media of hyping kids up. Kids play into the "hype" and then when the reality of college athletics hits, are culture shocked. Be humble, be confident in your skills, but never disregard hard work. Your skills get you noticed, your hard work gives you the opportunity to achieve success within your sport.

One of my favorite athletes, Kevin Durant, once said, "Hard work beats talent when talent fails to work hard." You can have tremendous talent, but hard work takes your game to the next level. An incredible work ethic will provide you with more opportunities than you can imagine, not only in the sports world, but in life. Competition at the college level is harder than most athletes think entering college.

Depending on what conference your school is competing in, most conferences are tougher than others. Within the world of college athletics, colleges that identify themselves in the NCAA are usually from division I, II, and III. Most athletes aim to compete at the division I level because it is the most intense level. After division I follows division II and then division III.

Not everybody gets a shot at the division I level, but that doesn't always mean the athlete was terrible or not athletically gifted. There could be numerous reasons as to why an athlete who has the potential to play at that level does not end up getting that opportunity immediately:

1. **High school GPA or ACT/SAT Scores**: Most of the time, athletes don't get an opportunity at a division I scholarship because they had an exceptionally low GPA in high school or they've failed the required courses in high school to prepare for college. Another reason can be not taking the SAT/ACT in time to gather and analyze scores, or not doing well and having bad scores. That is why as an athlete, if you already know that you want to compete in athletics at the college level, you must prepare in high school because grades matter. At the end of the day, that is the only way you can be accepted into college, no matter what type of scholarship is offered to you.

2. **Exposure:** Most high school athletes do not get the proper exposure for certain coaches to see them play their sport for recruitment opportunities. For example: If you went to a high school that is not commonly known for their sports program and you do not participate in any summer leagues or summer select teams, or other teams outside of your school teams, chances are you

won't have the opportunity to be seen by coaches that are looking to recruit. Some kids might not participate in AAU basketball for instance, because they or their parents can't afford to pay all the fees needed to play on a team or it is hard for them to get to practices because their parents work. For others, it can be that they are not on the right team that participates in certain tournaments that most coaches attend or maybe they are not introducing your name to coaches on the list of players to watch.

3. Talent Level: When getting recruited, coaches look at multiple things and not just your athletic talent. But at the end of the day, your athletic abilities earn you that scholarship. They want to recruit an athlete that is going to help them not only win games but championships as well. Every coach wants to win, and they must recruit accordingly. They sometimes pass up on certain athletes because they believe that they are not yet ready to compete at that level.

4. Not enough scholarships: Schools are required to award a certain number of scholarships per year. They must analyze the number of athletes currently on the team and the number of athletes that are going to be graduating soon. Coaches also recruit in advance, so there are scholarships offered to athletes who are not yet seniors in high school.

5. Already have the people they want: Most coaches might be at a point where they have already recruited the athletes they want and are no longer looking for recruits.

There are times where you'll be tested. Your mind, abilities, love for the sport, body, and aspirations for the sport will be tested. The secret to dealing with it is to acquire a mindset that brings you back to why you are playing the sport you chose. Most athletes want an opportunity at the next level, and for some, it is their sport paying for college, so they stay motivated to be able to obtain that scholarship. Being able to be motivated and driven really depends on what type of person you are as well as the type of background you come from.

For example, someone that came from a tougher background might hold up differently than someone who had opportunities growing up. Your upbringing and the environment you are around shapes you and molds you into the type of person you are and could possibly be. Of course, people sometimes reject the environment and influence they come from and turn to their own path. It is also possible to grow up a certain way and make a change and become someone different. Though we have many influences and things confronting us from different angles daily, we still should stay true to ourselves and live for ourselves. Never feel pressured to do anything that is out of character just because everyone else is doing it or because it is the "popular" thing to do at the moment.

I believe in individuality and significant uniqueness in everyone. People are different for a reason. You are to remain yourself and not try and clone anyone else because that's when unhappiness and dissatisfaction begin. You can never truly master being someone else.

We see athletes compete well in high school and think, oh yes, he is good, he will be recruited by the "BIG" schools. It is not where everybody else thinks you should go, it is where you think you will be most valuable and will play the most that you should go.

With so many talented athletes today, obtaining a scholarship has gotten increasingly competitive. To set yourself apart so that you get noticed by college coaches and athletic programs, always work on something that nobody else has so you are more valuable. Do not try and become a shooter only because that's what everyone considers themselves nowadays. Work on a skill that you have that you are good at and expand it, so you can get more exposure. It will set you apart from the norm and the uniqueness of your skill will get you noticed.

My rule of thumb is, admire those athletes that you consider your role models from afar, incorporate their work into yours, but always remain yourself and never change your game to fit theirs because you want to be like them. Make your game fit you and that will set you apart. I would never try and be another Candace Parker because there is already a Candace Parker. There are some things she probably took from some people to incorporate in her game, but at the end of the day, there are some things we take from her because those are the things she does well. It is called the evolution of basketball and greatness. You admire, you incorporate, but you also be you and stay true to yourself, so you may leave a legacy of your own.

Always remember that college student-athletes are going to be just as good as you, or even better. The goal is not to expect nor feel obligated to a starting position. The goal is to work hard, perfect your craft, learn from your experienced teammates, and be ready for when your time comes.

There's a misconception by the players that the coaches are expected to give them a starting position when they get to college. When you are recruited out of high school, you are recruited because coaches see potential in you. There will rarely be a player that is recruited and has all the necessary skills. It takes time and work to develop your skills to be the player you are meant to be.

To limit these expectations that they will hold a starting position when they get to college, coaches should be honest. Maybe say something like , "You are good, and I want you on my team. I see a lot of potential in you and with hard work I think you can help us achieve some goals we have set for the team. What I need you to do is to work hard, play hard, work on perfecting your skills, make yourself better so you can make your teammates better. Learn from the team elders to get an understanding of how it all works and leave the playing time to me. Control what you can control, and I will control the rest. As you know, you might not be the only significant player on the team, but I can see you making us better and having a significant role as well as helping us reach some of those goals we set for ourselves to help our team achieve as much as possible."

If a coach were to tell me this instead of lying to me and telling me everything I need to hear to make me commit, I would have more respect for that coach. I would play hard because we established a sense of trust. I would know there were good intentions for me because the coach was real enough to tell me the truth. If you are not getting enough playing, it is best that you try to talk to your teammates to see what the coach sees during practice that you don't see.

For most coaches, if you cannot perform during practice and do what they tell you to do, they won't trust you to do it in a game. The key is to practice like you're playing a game. Show your coach exactly how you will handle game-like situations and that you can play and play hard.

Most athletes think coaches limit them. Sometimes that can be true, but athletes limit themselves as well. They trap themselves in a belief that the coach is implying that I am not good enough and end up losing confidence in themselves and their abilities. The thing that ruins some athletes and sometimes drives them towards transferring is letting negative thoughts consume their minds.

They don't know how to let go of those thoughts or outgrow that mindset. There was an incredibly good coach of mine, Kasondra Foreman, who once said, "Don't let someone who didn't give you the game take everything away that the game has to offer you." If she had told me this when I was in college and not after, I would have been a different player. Sometimes as athletes, we let our coaches get to us. We let them control our minds so much that we end up losing our confidence in ourselves. We tend to cripple ourselves and believe we are not good enough and thus treat ourselves that way.

We sometimes do not rise above and get better on our own and change our circumstances and our mindset. I am a true believer in your mindset and outlook at the situation changing your circumstance.

When I was in college, I read a book by Carol S. Dweck, a Ph.D. psychology professor, called "Mindset. The New Psychology of Success". In her book, she mentioned two types of mindsets. One was the fixed mindset and the other was the growth mindset. She stated that the difference between the two is how you respond to situations after they've happened.

"The view you adopt for yourself profoundly affects the way you lead your life. It can determine whether you become the person you want to be and whether you accomplish the things you value." In other words, how you view yourself and your situations or circumstances can determine how you move and the type of decisions you make, thus leading you through a journey or path that lines up with those past decisions and possibly also shaping you into that person that fits that mindset you acquire for yourself.

She wrote, "The fixed mindset creates an urgency to prove yourself over and over. The growth mindset is based on the belief that your basic qualities are things you can cultivate through your efforts." She also believed that no matter your background, past experiences, or the journey you are currently on, you are always able to change your mindset to one or the other.

Let's look at some examples and take a closer look at the two mindsets. Let's use the example of playing time in college sports. Suppose that you never get playing time or your coach does not play you with the minutes you desire. With the two different mindsets, two different athletes will respond in two separate ways.

Athlete A with the fixed mindset will feel like a failure and try and correlate their lack of minutes directly to their competence level and worth. Their coping styles deal with self-criticism in a way that is unhealthy and can resort to the worst possible decisions or thoughts. These are the athletes that automatically think of transferring when these types of situations occur. Playing time doesn't always mean that you are not a talented player. A lot of reasons factor into playing time such as attitude in practice, your character on and off the court, how you treat your teammates and coaches and how hard you work day in and day out.

Athlete B with the growth mindset will acknowledge the fact and tell themselves they will have to work harder to get what they want. Growth mindset athletes closely look at the situation at hand, which is playing time, and consider workable solutions that can resolve their issues. The point is not to tell the athlete they should not be upset with the situation. The point is to help the athlete acknowledge and understand that it is upsetting and discover what to do moving forward to resolve their issue to win and get what they want in the end.

If a coach is not playing you, or you feel he doesn't like you for whatever reason, find out what you can do to make your situation better. If it means spending more time in the gym or extra time on the field every day on your own and working on moves or improving your speed, then that's what you do. If that means respectfully meeting with your coach and asking what you can do so you and the team could be better, then so be it.

My first year in college, I did not play as much as I thought and expected to play. This did not only upset me, but it also lit a fire under me. I was always that type of player that valued hard work and refining my skills as well as changing my circumstances, if presented with the opportunity. The first year became a learning experience for me. I took everything the coaches were saying, some of what the players were saying, how I felt due to limited minutes, and hit the gym hard every day.

I would be in the gym late at night around midnight until maybe one o'clock in the morning shooting and working on my moves. Whenever I got the opportunity during the day or after study hall, I would be in the gym working. It helped that I had a great teammate that had the same mindset and work ethic as me. We would be at the Rec (recreational center) playing with the boys and in the gym at night perfecting our crafts. It also helped that our practice gym was open 24/7 and that we had the key to get in.

After my first year, I got a trainer and worked out all summer. Everything I was uncomfortable with doing in practice or maybe did not do correctly, I worked on during the summer. Most people will not believe this but, I was in the gym every day with my trainer from maybe nine in the morning until nine at night. This is what you call a grind shift. Of course, I was tired and sometimes wanted to rest, but my love and determination for the sport overpowered how I felt about rest.

When I came back my sophomore year, not only did I earn a starting position, but I was snatching double doubles left and right. I took it upon myself to change my perspective and outlook and changed my circumstance. I did not sit around and accept what I was given. I loved the sport enough and knew I had the abilities and talent to play, so I made it happen. I doubt coaches are going to deny you playing time if you are good and can help them win games because their jobs are on the line.

There are some circumstances where the relationship between the coach and athlete is the result of limited to no playing time, and these cases are more prevalent than you know. If you follow the rules, you compete hard and practice hard, your chances are great. If you believe you've done everything in your power to make your situation better, but it doesn't get better, then maybe at that point you might start considering other opportunities. Find someone you trust and that is invested in you and your success and get their opinion and look at your options. You have to find a way and take the initiative and accountability of changing your circumstance and situation to make you happy.

You cannot rely on your coaches to make the situation better for you. Coaches have a lot on their plate sometimes and are pulled in different directions. They have fifteen plus players to care for, and if you do not take care of your business, they will not sit there and baby you until you feel good about yourself and your abilities.

Always be confident and believe in yourself and your abilities. When things are not going the way that you think they should for you, do not always consider the extremes and start thinking of transferring. Take the time to explore solutions to make your situation better. If it is not a healthy situation and you've tried everything possible, then maybe transferring might be the option for you. If someone does not give you the opportunity, create it yourself and watch your life change. Acquire a different outlook and watch your situation turn into an opportunity for something bigger or even better.

Remember with the fixed mindset, you are prone to avoid challenges, give up easily or get defensive, see effort as useless, ignore negative useful feedback, and feel threatened by the success of others thus, making it hard for you to reach your full potential. In contrast to the fixed mindset, athletes with the growth mindset are most likely able to embrace challenges, persist with setbacks, see effort as the path to proficiency, learn from criticism, and find lessons and inspirations in the success of others, providing them with the efforts to reach an elevated level of achievements. Remember, you are not stuck with one mindset. You can always change your mindset at any time and during any journey. Which mindset best reflects the type of person and athlete you are?

Someone once told me, "I think players should evaluate themselves. How they are doing in practices. Do they know all the plays, are they spending additional time in the gym outside of practice to improve themselves? If they are doing these things, they should take that step of setting a meeting with their coach to find out what else they can do to earn playing time."

Norrisha Victrum writes, "The competition was a lot different coming from high school. The speed and pace of the game was faster, the players were bigger, and they had players who were better, but you still have to find a way to score on them and contain them on defense. You have to study the game and scout each player and team you will be going against. I adjusted to the competition well. My first year I was thrown to the wolves because my senior point guard got kicked off, so I had to step up but didn't score like I did in high school. It took me until my junior year for me to be comfortable on the court."

Alexis Hyder describes her situation, "The competition from high school to college was significantly different because the commitment to the game had increased. In college you put in at least 20 hours a week towards your craft, in high school you were just doing it for fun. Adjusting was not hard based on the competition, it was the scouting and coaching staff that I needed adjustment to."

CHAPTER 7

Coaches' expectations

As a collegiate athlete or a high school athlete trying to get recruited by college coaches, you can expect these college coaches to have expectations and standards that they require you to meet. Most of these expectations are not negotiable and don't solely rely on your talent alone. The misconception most athletes have is that talent will take them where they need to go. As college coaches recruit or analyze their college players, they tend to look at other factors that contribute to the type of player you are and the type of player they want you to be for that program. The reason why coaches require lofty expectations of their athletes is because athletes not only represent themselves, but their university as well. You represent the program and not just yourself.

We can all agree that the talent level is rising within kids coming out of high school and even athletes finding their niche in college and fulfilling their potential. With the numerous talents around us, you must be aware and control what you can control. Consider how you will set yourself apart from everybody else competing for the same spot that you are competing for. You should look to gain and understand the different attributes coaches look for outside of pure talent. Here are the five main attributes coaches look for in athletes they want to coach:

1. **Work Ethic**. You can be as talented as

ever, but if your work ethic is nonexistent, they will not look to recruit you or even play you. Coaches want to see an athlete that works hard on and off the field, someone who will give it their all and go hard. They want to see determination, and someone who is willing to work on themselves to improve themselves. A strong work ethic shows toughness, and it also shows that no matter what your strengths or weaknesses are, you are willing to go hard every day despite the talent you may lack in certain areas. For example: Let's say we have two athletes. Athlete A has some talent but rarely works hard. Athlete B is mediocre but possesses a lot of heart and excellent work ethic. Here is the thought process of a coach. Coaches do not want to take many risks. Their jobs are on the line and they don't want to waste scholarships on athletes they know will not impact their programs positively. If the choice is between an athlete who has talent but doesn't work hard and is lazy and only depends on their talent when it's game time to win versus an athlete who has some talent, lacks in a few areas, but is willing to dive on the floor for loose balls, take charges, grab rebounds, play defense, and always give it their best, the choice is easy and simple. Coaches without a doubt would choose the athlete that does the dirty work and has a strong work ethic. You can improve talent and tweak it to fit their style of play, you cannot teach work ethic. And they certainly do not have time to babysit an athlete and beg them to have a work ethic they are expected to already have.

2.   Athletes must be **coachable**. As an

athlete, your game is going to be criticized. There is no athlete that doesn't get criticism for the way they play or do things on the court or field. What athletes need to understand is where this criticism is coming from. There is a difference between people criticizing you because they don't necessarily like your game and people criticizing you because they want you to be great and want to help expand and improve your game. You must gauge the information you are being told and understand from whom, so you know how to apply it. As an athlete, whether you agree with your coach's criticism or not, you must take it and show respect when they are advising you on something. Being coachable shows your willingness and eagerness to learn and hear people out on what they might see that you don't. We athletes aren't real with ourselves sometimes and believe that we are perfect players. There is no such thing as a perfect player or athlete. We must open ourselves up for criticism and be able to take coaching and apply it, so we improve ourselves to reach our destinations. You must show that you can listen, understand what they are saying, and apply to the areas of your abilities that they believe you can improve on. It is okay to have a conversation or discussion of what they are asking you to do, but never close them out and automatically think they are wrong or trying to criticize you. What we ourselves don't see, others see. No coach wants an athlete that is tremendously talented but isn't coachable and always has something to respond.

3. Be a **leader**. A leader is someone who

leads a team and guides them to whatever goal they are trying to accomplish as a team and individually. They encourage their teammates to do their jobs and keep them on task. They lead by example and are all about the team. Leaders do not have time to be selfish. They aim for success and motivate everyone around them to be successful. To be honest, not everyone is a leader and not everyone is comfortable with being a leader. I don't think there is anything wrong with being a follower if you are following the leader on the team. When coaches try to "force" certain athletes that do not have the ability nor the personality to lead, the dynamic of the team doesn't turn out to be what they want it or expect it to be. Being a leader shouldn't be assigned by "seniority" and it shouldn't be assigned because you are the best player on the team. The title "leader" should only be assigned to those that possess those characteristics. Coaches want to see that you are more interested in the team than you are in yourself. They want to know that you care about the success of the team and if you do not get your stats that you are still okay with the outcome. If you are one of those athletes that thinks they are not a leader and will never fill that role, that is okay. Just make sure to be the best follower you can be and do everything that you are asked of by your leader. Trust your leader and help them make their jobs a little easier. Leaders deal with a lot of tasks and responsibility. You must be ready always to speak up to your teammates and do what's right.

4.   Must be a **team player**. We as athletes

sometimes get so caught up in our own world that we forget we have people by our sides that are there to make our jobs easier. We tend to take everything on ourselves and feel as if we must save the day. We focus too much on stats, and while that is important, without wins nobody will ever know your stats or who you are. You must be a team player and put the team first and yourself second. The most successful programs are the programs where everybody on the team knows their roles, accepts their roles, plays their roles well, and puts the team's success ahead of their own. Without wins, championships, or conference titles, you as the athlete will never get the exposure you need to get the opportunity to play at the next level. This is easier said than done, but I believe every athlete struggles with this. I struggled with this in college because as much as I wanted my team to win, I was also worried about my stat line and how it looked on paper. Most nights I would give myself personal goals instead of team goals. Being a team player is involving your teammates in plays and not trying to make it difficult on yourself trying to fulfill a certain stat line. Stats are recognized when the team is recognized.

5. Have good **character and attitude**. Coaches don't teach character and attitude and will never dedicate their time to do so. If you have a bad attitude, you will certainly struggle not only in your sport but in life. Coaches can tell the type of person you are by your character and the attitude you display. Our sports make us passionate at times, but don't ever let it take you out of your character. Coaches want to know if they can trust, depend, and

rely on you to get the job done when they need you to. They also want to know if you are going to do it with a good attitude or complain about it. Never expect to be babied by college coaches. They are not there to tell you everything is all right, that's what your parents are for. They are there to criticize, motivate, and help you reach your full potential whether it's positive some days or negative other days. I believe as athletes, we are so quick to judge our coaches sometimes and believe they have something against us. What we need to do is also analyze ourselves, take a step back, and see if there is something we see or something we are doing wrong that is causing them to act the way they do or might do.

Whether you are aware coaches are looking for these qualities or not, they are. They won't take a chance on someone they know will cause problems and will waste their time. Most of the attributes listed are not taught. They are things you should already have as an athlete. You should always want to display your best self around coaches. Don't be afraid to be yourself, but also know what is appropriate and what is not.

At the end of the day, they have the ability and power to pass you up and not provide you with a scholarship. They can take your scholarship away. Never put your scholarship at risk because you have an attitude problem or refuse to be coachable. Remember, you do not represent yourself only, but your team as well. There is a reason why the school's name is at the front of the jersey and your name at the back.

CHAPTER 8

Athletes' expectations

Just as coaches have expectations for athletes, athletes have expectations of coaches. Athletes care about what their coaches say and think and value the information given them, however, there is a difference between getting it from someone you know who cares about you, your growth, and success as opposed to someone who doesn't. It is important as coaches to create individualize relationships with your athletes and not generalize to everyone. Athletes want their coaches to be leaders, honest, invested, fair, mentors, and someone they can trust.

Most people do not understand or know this, but an athlete's overall performance is based on the coach and his or her actions or expectations of that athlete. I saw this happen many times in college throughout my four years. There are some players that get recruited and then turn out to be opposite of what the coach expected them to be. The reason for this is the fact that coaches don't understand that not all athletes are able to automatically adjust to the competition of college athletics.

The level of competition in college athletics is not easy because athletes are basically competing with other athletes that are either of their caliber or better. So, if you come from a school that did not have the most talented district to play against, adjusting to real competition when you get to college might be challenging for some. The coaches' job in that situation is not to automatically assume the athletes are not good and not who they expected them to be. Coaches need to find out why they are struggling, coach them on how they can improve and then support them while they undergo that transition from being the best player on their previous team to earning playing time now at the college level.

I knew an athlete that came in as a freshman at the forward position at her university. As a freshman student coming in, there is so much pressure to perform and prove to the coaching staff that they indeed recruited a talented player. In some programs, most of the junior and senior girls do not really welcome the freshmen's and tend to treat them badly since they see them as a threat to keeping their starting positions and playing time.

During drills, the freshman showed signs of a lack of confidence in herself and her abilities, which played out negatively in the coach's eyes. She was overshadowed and didn't really get enough playing time the first half of her career because the coach thought she was uncapable of accomplishing what needed to be done on the court. The coach didn't realize her potential or all the skills she could provide the team.

When a new coach came in, she got moved to a different position, showed talents the new coach knew she had, and became the best mid-range shooter on the team. She could shoot all along, but because she was playing the wrong position, she couldn't really show her other skill sets. With the new coach's confidence in her, she grew tremendous confidence in herself and never doubted to shoot the ball. She found the joy of the game again.

Most times, coaches get so caught up in positions that they overlook some qualities athletes have that may be outside of their designated roles coming out of high school. Other times, coaches will recruit one way but won't develop the athlete into other roles where they might be successful.

I believe it takes the right coach to bring out the greatness in an athlete. Athletes can try and try on their own, but the right coach can provide them with confidence that can fuel the potential that each athlete possess. What your coach thinks of you as a player reflects in the way that you play. If a coach has tremendous confidence in you and they trust you, you will play with confidence. If a coach does not have confidence in you and expects you to always mess up, it will show, and you will play without confidence and scared, thus making more mistakes along the way.

Coaches sometimes have a pride factor that they do not want to let go of regarding a specific athlete. Most are not able to change their beliefs. They try to apply the same coaching styles to every athlete. It is said that the athlete is supposed to adjust to the coach, but I think they are both supposed to adjust to each other. For example, there are times when an athlete is playing for a coach who did not recruit them. It makes it tough on the athlete as well as the coach. In these instances, both sides are uncomfortable with the fact that they did not get who they wanted.

Athletes will try to prove themselves to the coach that they are good enough, but sometimes coaches make up their mind that this is not the athlete they recruited and do not trust to play for them. What usually happens after that is, the athlete either tries to transfer or stays and has a terrible experience. Sometimes, coaches will bluntly tell an athlete to transfer and then present them with possible options of where they can transfer and finish out their playing careers.

Here are some things that athletes expect from their coaches:

1.   **Trust.** Athletes want coaches they can trust and who won't lie to them. It is better to be upfront and honest with the athlete, so they are aware of what's going on. It makes no sense to lie to an athlete about playing time, position, or the role they play on the team. Being honest with an athlete opens a line of communication and allows the athlete to truly listen and value the coach and everything that is said by the coach. It also helps the athlete determine their next steps and realize what they might have been doing wrong and fix it.

2.   **Fair.** Athletes want coaches that coach everyone in the same manner. They want a fair chance at the same position. Although most coaches say that they don't typically have favorites, we all know that is not true. With regard to personality, I think as a coach, you are certainly not going to connect with every one of your athletes on the team the same way. It is possible to be more drawn to certain people, just as athletes typically are drawn to certain coaches on the staff. The goal is to have mutual respect and treat them the same in practice and games as you do your "favorite" players or the athletes you better connect with because of their personalities or character.

3.   **Invested.** Every athlete desires a coach that is and will be invested in them. They want a coach that sees their vision and potential and then wants to help them achieve that vision. This vision doesn't always have to be an athletic vision, it can sometimes be academic as well. To know that your coaches fully support you is the greatest feeling an athlete can have.

As a coach, your perspective must take on a different lens when dealing with your athletes. You should always invest in your athletes both as an athlete and as a person. An athlete should not go into your program or university and graduate the same person. The purpose of the four years is to grow as an athlete and as a person. If they come out the same as they went in, you did not do your job correctly as a coach. As a coach, you have the toughest, most interesting, and rewarding job there is to have. You have the opportunity to educate, mold, and build character within your athletes. You possess the ability to change lives and invest greatness into your athletes. If you see it as a job and position, that is all it's ever going to be, but if you see it as a tool to help young adults prepare for the "real world", then you're using the right lens. Most coaches come from athletic backgrounds. Treat your athletes how you would have wanted to be treated when you were at that level. When you look at it that way, your perception should change. There is a beautiful quote by Felicia Hall-Allen, a very prominent speaker and mentor in women's basketball, who said, "Be a GIVER instead of a GETTER when you believe in the beauty of someone else's dream. That is how you impact their lives forever." It is important to always believe beyond what you see, as your athletes can always surprise you

CHAPTER 9

Day in the life

The life of a student athlete is planned from the time they wake up to the time they go to sleep. From the first year to senior year, athletes juggle school, athletics, and social lives. Your classes are planned around your athletics and your social lives are planned around athletics and your classes.

Your schedules during the summer are a little bit different than your schedules in the fall when school officially starts. You have more to manage during the fall because you are required to take a certain number of hours and pre-season starts for those sports that are in season during that time.

"At times it was great", said Aluk Adub. "My teammates and I outside of practice lived life. The down part sometimes was never having the time to socialize. Everything was school and basketball. If there was an event going on at school, you couldn't make it because you are either at practice or you had to wake up at 6:00am for weights. That is the price we pay, and we end up paying more of the price than regular students at times."

"Every day was a new challenge whether it was getting in from a road game at one o'clock in the morning, attending class at 9:00 am or the internal battles with myself when dealing with coaches. During my 4 years of college, I had 3 different head coaches and adjusting to them was difficult for me. Being mentally, physically, and emotionally exhausted and still having to push everyday was also something I battled with", said Kasiney Williams.

"It was tough coming back from an away game at 3:00 am having class the next morning at 8:00am with a hurt ankle", said Aluk. "Not being able to pick out the schedule you want for classes and having a limit on a major you want to do because it interfered with basketball was tough also"

Statements like these help you realize that being a student athlete is tough because your time is planned according to your sport and your classes. You might wake up and have weights and then go to class and then maybe have practice later that day. Because of our sport and the various competitions, we travel to, we as student athletes are provided with tutoring sessions at a facility provided by the athletic department to ensure we are always caught up and not missing any school work or important exams and tests.

I know when I was in school my first year, they required a certain number of study hall hours a week whether you had a session with a tutor or not. Over time, they realized that some students had good grades and gave them that flexibility of coming for extra time if they needed but they did not have to come in unless they had tutoring sessions. This was a good thing because it motivated certain athletes to bring up their GPAs, so they wouldn't have to be in study hall by themselves. Of course, everybody wants time to themselves, so it encouraged a lot of GPAs to rise. I personally liked study hall because it forced me to stay in one space where I had the tools to finish my work and then go home and head to bed.

Traveling for competition was probably the hardest thing to do in college. You missed out on a lot of in-class activities and had to make them up whenever you got back. Some people might think that professors are usually fond of athletes but not every one of them is. Some professors do not care about your athletic status and will treat you like any other student.

We should not get special treatment as athletes, but it is important for professors to understand our schedules and help figure out a solution make up the school work we missed that day or that week, depending on what type of competition it was. Sometimes we would come back from competition and have study hall that same day. Other times we would come back early in the morning and go to class tired and burnt out.

As an athlete, you really have to understand the level at which you are competing and have to measure up. There are some difficulties, but you have to be tough enough to be able to deal with it all and still come out victorious. You must be able to apply yourself and make sure you are taking care of yourself and your work during the midst of the work storms you might experience.

To provide a better visual of a typical day in the life of an athlete, here is an example of when I was in school. Summer schedules are quite different than the fall and spring schedules. It's more laid back in the summer and you have more time because you are not taking that many classes, maybe two at the most. Most of your workouts are geared towards the morning and some in the afternoon so you have the rest of your day unless you have community service planned for that day by the team or you have night class or labs that you might have to attend.

As a college athlete, you are required to take a minimum of 12 credit hours each semester to maintain NCAA eligibility. To complete your degree within four years, you must average 15 credits per semester in most academic programs. At the University of North Texas, I took 15 hours every semester. A typical day required me waking up, attending weights, and conditioning that morning around 6:00am. After weights and conditioning, I rushed to class because I had 8:00am classes up until my junior year of college. This may sound nasty. I would not have time to take a shower and properly prepare myself for class, so I would rush back to the dorm, pick up my books and backpack, grab a deodorant stick, and head straight to class.

We were expected to be in class on time and sit in the first three rows. I had no problem with the front row situation. I think you learn better and participation is easier when you are closer to the professor. Distractions are also limited because you are close enough that they can see and hear everything you do. Since we were required to sit in the first three rows, I would try and grab a seat in an area where it was somewhat empty. I didn't feel comfortable sitting near students who had adequate time to get ready for class. I was sweaty and tired from the workout I just endured and just wanted some air. Those seats in college are so close, it's astounding.

Usually after class or some classes, I would head over to the gym to get taped and prepare for practice. Most of the time, depending on when practice was, I did not have time to grab lunch before the practice. The neat thing is, they would have this snack bar set up for us to grab something to digest right before practice. Obviously, it wasn't a five-course meal because you had workouts, but it helped with the hunger and it wasn't too heavy to bear in practice. After practice, I would head back to my room to get ready for study hall.

Most of the time, depending on how long practice was, I would just go straight from practice without showering because being late to study hall was not an option. Frequently, I had time to enjoy my shower and grab something quick to eat before study hall. That all depended on the end of practice time and the beginning of my tutoring sessions. After study hall, if I was able to complete all my homework and study sessions after my tutoring sessions in study hall, I would be able to go home, shower, eat dinner and lay down for the night.

If not and the homework was due that night or I had an exam to take that night, I would hurry home, complete the homework or exam, and then proceed to shower, eat, and then call it a day. Every morning, I would wake up and do the same thing again. Most days were busier than others, but their patterns were all the same in the end.

The most important thing to take away from this is time management. Although everything is technically already planned out for you, you still need to manage your time accordingly. If you do not, you will fall through the cracks and it will be hard for you to cope with everything that is thrown at you daily.

Always be sure to take care of yourself. In retrospect, I should have taken care of myself a little bit more. I didn't have to basically starve myself until the end of the day to eat. I could have packed lunch or could have gotten my friends to bring me some. When I'm in work mode or when I'm busy or have a lot of stuff to do, I get so concerned with finishing those tasks that I completely forget about myself and what I may need to be able to complete those things successfully.

CHAPTER 10

Social media love

Social media is more prevalent today than it has ever been. Most of the information we need is on social media now. Just because it is on social media though, does not mean that it is true or factual. What you put out there is for public viewing and is never truly private. Most athletes use social media intelligently and others use it negatively. As you may already know, nothing is ever private on the internet whether your account is private or not.

The effects of social media can be positive, but they can also be negative. As a student athlete, it is wise to not only monitor what you put on social media, but also how others interact with you on social media. If you are in high school, it is important because college coaches check social media to gain information on their recruits and to see the various extremes of their personalities and character. Since most student athletes getting recruited do not speak much about their lives outside of their sport due to shyness, coaches check social media to see if they can get extra information that will help them with understanding the type of person and athlete they might possibly have to deal with.

College coaches will not recruit or take a chance on an athlete that could possibly ruin the image of their university and athletic program. They not only protect the university's image but theirs as well. Their jobs are on the line and they look for athletes that are going to help them and not hinder the program's success or their success within their roles.

Just as there are difficult college coaches, there are difficult athletes as well. Take a few minutes to analyze yourself and see what kind of an athlete you are and what type of athlete you want to be known as. As a student athlete, you are scrutinized by many people. That is why coaches often stress the importance of positive self-image. The reason is because of the amount of attention athletic programs receive. It is imperative that student athletes not only reflect a positive image of themselves, but of the program as well.

If you are an athlete already in college, it is vital that your social media account reflects professionalism and appropriate behavior because, again, you not only represent yourself but also your university or college, and your athletic program. With that in mind, make sure you are aware of what you post and how you post it on social media. What you consider private is not necessarily private. What you consider innocent and harmless might be interpreted differently than how you intended it to be. Things are consistently taken out of context all the time on social media. People read posts and tweets from different points of view, and a simple song lyric might even be taken out of context and viewed negatively.

The most important thing to examine when using social media is the content you are posting and your motives behind that content. Social media can be a great tool to use in terms of exposure or for branding purposes. When used negatively, it can ruin images and limit, cancel, and eliminate any possible opportunities in getting recruited. It can put your scholarship at risk.

With social media, there are some advantages and disadvantages. Some advantages include but are not limited to making connections with coaches, exposure to the athletic world for recruiting purposes, branding yourself, providing a channel of communication with others, and as a way to connect with your fans. Some disadvantages include loss of focus and various distractions, potential loss of scholarships, and ruined reputations.

Advice for using social media as an athlete includes following the right people, monitoring what you say and how you say it, and remembering that you are not just representing yourself and what you attach yourself to plays a role in the kind of person you are branding, yourself to be and how others perceive you. Everything you do on social media relates back to the type of person you are and can either be a good thing or terrible thing depending on the athlete and their motives.

Social media usage is not only important for coaches and the athletic world, but also professional companies that you may work for in the future that also might view your social media accounts. Being an athlete is not forever and someday you will enter the work world or work with brands for those that end up going professional. What you do now can and will affect you at a later time.

When you graduate, most of you will enter the work world and apply for jobs. Your resume is good, but when companies do their research and they see that your social media accounts are unsuitable, they will pass you.

It is wise to be cautious with the type of content you put out in the digital world. There are some athletes that do not care what they post or who they interact with on social media. If you care about your self-image and care about not taking away future opportunities for yourself, do the right thing and avoid actions with negative outcomes. I think it is great that we express our personalities and likes on social media. I think that is what brings communities together. But negativity exists on social media and it is smart to exclude yourself from it and make sure you are the one who is always positive and representing yourself well.

By no means am I saying to be fake on social media so people see you a certain way, but you must discern what you can and cannot show the world, especially in the type of position you're in. Not everything is for public viewing. Whether you know it or not, you will always have people watching you as an athlete and you may never know exactly who it is and how they could have impacted your life. Never post when you are emotional and consider a post multiple times before posting. If you have to ask yourself if it is appropriate, nine times out of ten it is not, so do not post it.

Just as social media can provide you a platform to be yourself and express your interests, it can also be an extremely dangerous and a scary place. I had the opportunity of interviewing Manyang "Manny" Chan all the way from Melbourne, Australia. Manny founded a club called "The Longhorns Basketball Club" which is a big club in Australia that mentors and helps kids that have a passion for the sport of basketball come to the United States and pursue their dreams of going to high school, college and then the pros. Many of these kids from Australia are originally Sudanese.

Manny said, "Social media is really big now. It connects the sports world worldwide. Media accounts such as YouTube, Facebook, Twitter and even Instagram give kids the opportunity to post and showcase themselves all the way from Australia. I think the United States really knows how to market themselves in sports, especially the NBA. Kids are looking at these NBA games on TV and then automatically aspiring to make it there one day."

The NBA has become a global game and kids from all over the world long for the opportunity to make it there one day. It most certainly influences a lot of kids and makes a lot of them want to play at the college level, so they can have a chance at the pro level. "For kids in the States, their journey is a lot easier than international kids that try to come to the States to maybe get a shot at the same opportunity.

The sad thing for Australians is that there is a whole lot of work that goes into the process of coming to the States to get a shot at the high school or college level." He said. Coaches just don't go to Australia to recruit. They barely have time to go and see their own recruits here in the States. What Sudanese athletes from Australia do is go through a process of getting a visa to come to school here so that they might have better recruitment opportunities when it comes to obtaining scholarships to college. No matter the talent, if they live in Australia it is harder for them to get college scholarship opportunities than those athletes that already live in the States and have crazy amounts of exposure. Their main reason for these moves is exposure purposes and a shot at their dreams.

"They want to attend high school in the States and not just college or the pros because they want to grow within the system and enhance their skills as well as learn how to play with the Americans since they will potentially be their teammates or opponents.

Most of you are familiar with Ben Simmons who is now in the league. Ben is originally from Australia and decided to complete his final two years in the States before attending LSU followed by the NBA shortly after. The path that Ben took is exactly what kids in Australia try to do. The really negative and scary part of this process of kids coming from Australia is that there are people and even some coaches that are ready to exploit these kids for their own personal gains because some athletes have promising talents or just do not know a lot about the process and are unaware of what they need to look out for."

Referencing it back to social media, there are coaches that may sometimes put kids in bad situations because they promise them certain things due to their potential in their sport. With social media big nowadays and more athletes taking advantage of it for exposure purposes, more coaches are recruiting via social media and these international kids are falling for it because of their mindset of chasing their dreams no matter what.

"Kids get caught up in the hype in trying to get their dreams come true," Manny said. "I've witnessed these situations for myself with kids in my program. Coaches will see these posts of games and highlights from the athletes, reach out to them, tell these kids that they will get them in AAU tournaments to get exposure and that they will make it into the NBA and that they will set them up. So, what these kids do in return is get tourist visas and think that they can survive on that in the States and be able to attend schools or participate in whatever else these coaches are promising kids."

"A V2 visa here in Australia will only give you 90 days in the States and on that 89th day, you must be on your way back to Australia or you will be facing problems. The Australian kids are given the wrong advice and are getting the wrong ideas on how to go about this entire process of making their dreams come true. They are being ripped off and that is something that is unfair to the athletes and parents that fund these opportunities for their athletes. Since most of our kids are Sudanese and most of their parents are uninvolved due to their lack of knowledge of the athletic world, these kids are making the decision on their own."

Athletes will do anything to chase their dreams and make them come true. There is nothing wrong with chasing your dreams, I think that is what life is all about. The most important thing to remember, though, is to chase them in a smart way. Be aware of your surroundings and the situations you might be getting yourself into. Social media can be a wonderful place, but it can also be unsafe and sometimes people can take advantage of you by posing as someone who possesses credibility. It is best that you have someone in your circle that can help you navigate through all the recruiting via social media and help you detect any red flags you might be blind to.

There is nothing more important than keeping yourself safe. Never compromise your livelihood in relation to chasing your dream. Always be careful, be wise and aware, and ask for advice from others you trust when people on social media reach out to you. Find credibility before you trust the coaches with your life.

CHAPTER 11

What is the hype about

With social media exposure comes what is known in the athletic world as the "hype." Hype is a level of admiration and praise given to certain athletes due to their athletic abilities and potential to be great within their sport. It is especially given to young players who are playing at a high level beyond their class and peers in their age group.

The rate at which athletes today are growing both physically and mentally is astonishing. Kids in middle school look older than they should and so do kids in high school. This is especially true with boys. I am not sure what parents today are feeding their kids, but it's something my parents should have fed me when I was in high school because I was small as ever. Kids are growing rapidly and if you combine that with the level of skill, knowledge of their sport, and physical training, athletes that are well rounded and more advanced than their peers are produced. They are required to meet certain expectations and achieve a certain level of success within their sport that they are not even prepared for.

When they fall short of those expectations or do not reach their full potential, they are supported less and are criticized not only by their peers but also by social media. The level of expectations required of these athletes may cause a lot of stress and distractions for certain athletes. Hype is not all bad. Depending on the type of athlete, how its handled can either be good or bad. There are a few athletes that are falsely hyped due to one game that went viral or because of who their parents are and who they know. Most frequently, kids are hyped due to the school that they committed or what their last name is.

There is nothing wrong with giving an athlete praise for their hard, consistent work, but do not ever over do it. Where you are now as an athlete is not where you are going to be in a few years. In time, athletes in your age range that might have been overlooked might develop skills of their own and pass you up on the list, if you become arrogant with a love of social media.

There are some advantages and disadvantages to the hype. One advantage of the hype is exposure and future scholarships opportunities. Disadvantages may include level of stress, not living up to the hype, injuries, circumstances, coach and player relationship, athletic programs, and social influences surrounding the athlete. How hype plays out depends on the athlete and how they view it. It also depends on the level of confidence they have within themselves and their abilities. Some athletes use this to their advantage and remain focused, competitive, humble, and still work hard to fulfill their own as well as other people's expectations of them and reach their full potential. Some athletes take it straight to the head and have a different demeanor regarding this. They start to think that they are invincible and untouchable and begin to lose focus on the mission, then struggle to perform to the best of their abilities when the time comes.

Whether you get a lot of hype or no hype at all, the "hype" does not necessarily validate anything about your game or skills. I know athletes that were hyped and didn't live up to it, and athletes that weren't and became phenomenal players. It is not how people see you that matters so much, but how you see yourself, where you see yourself, how you will get yourself to your goals, and the confidence that will fuel everything within you.

There is nothing wrong with expressing interest in an athlete or even admitting that their abilities are unique and great but there is a difference between admiration and exaggeration. The problem with this technique is that an athlete can get affected severely by this hype. Most athletes play into it, forgetting all aspects of hard work and then struggle to cope when they do not play up to the hype, or what they say, "live" up to the hype.

Kids are recruited as young as middle school and are pressured into this identity that they have not even grown into. They are rated by people that don't even play sports and only understand the surface level of it. They are given this "fame" because they may be the best athletes in their class at that time. They are rated and given a status when they are incredibly young, and people then wonder why some athletes do not live up to the hype. What people do not realize is, whether you are rated now or not, your skills are either going to expand and grow or they are going to stay stagnant. There are some athletes that aren't particularly good growing up, and out of nowhere become the best athletes you've ever seen. Michael Jordan got cut from his high school team growing up but yet, he became Michael Jordan.

Speaking from a basketball background, the game of basketball is uniquely beautiful. You can start off with having initial skills, or you can go into it completely without any type of skills and later discover them like I did. The game of basketball is all about hard work and repetition. The more you work on a move and the more you perfect it, the better your skills get. If you do not do anything, you stay stagnant and your skills do not expand.

Austin Mitchell says, "I feel like it is harder for athletes now because of social media. There is so much more pressure to perform and there are more opportunities too for people to compare athletes and rate them based on their athletic abilities. Athletes now have to deal with being liked more and are even under a bigger microscope."

The "hype" should not be the deciding factor when you believe that you are a talented player or not. As an athlete, you are always competing, against yourself and your peers. Never get complacent and do not let silly things such as "hype" dictate the type of player you should be or the type of person you should act like. Hype doesn't directly help you when it comes to game time because you must use your skills to prove you are worth the hype. If you are an athlete that is overlooked, the tables always turn at some point. If they don't love you now, they'll love you later.

Just keep up the work and don't play into social media and what people think of you. I say this because most of the time, you are being judged by people that can't even play the sport themselves. If that is who you choose to dictate the type of athlete you should be, you will have a tough time loving the type of athlete you are and succeeding in your career.

CHAPTER 12

Prep-schools and international athletes

Prep-schools exist because they operate outside of the state athletic association in the basketball world. Most athletes who attend prep-schools do so because they operate differently from traditional high schools and don't follow the same rules. Other athletes attend prep-schools for basketball purposes only with the intent on preparing for junior college and college sports. Another reason why athletes might attend a prep-school is because they did not have the proper grades in high school and need to do an extra year to get their grades where they need them to attend college and go on to play their sport.

Prep-schools are not just limited to in-state athletes but international athletes as well. In fact, international athletes are the ones that commonly take this route in hopes of receiving something beneficial to them in the end, such as potential exposure to college coaches and scouts. For athletes that reside in the U.S., recruitment is easy, and exposure is not as hard to obtain as it is for international kids. Due to this, international athletes go to the extremes of putting themselves in danger chasing their dreams of coming to the states to study and play the sport that they love.

The NBA is a global sport meaning it is not only viewed and recognized by athletes in the U.S, but international athletes as well. International kids that play basketball from their home countries see NBA games on TV and aspire to one day play for the league themselves. They make plans to come to the States to chase their dreams of attending high school and then receiving college athletic scholarships which they believe gives them the opportunity at the league in the future.

Manny, who is the coach of the Sudanese Longhorns basketball club in Melbourne, Australia, is familiar with athletes leaving Australia to come to the States to chase their dreams and sometimes end up in situations they did not intend on or plan for.

Throughout the interview, he mentions how the unspoken world of prep-schools play a Significant role in an athlete's life, especially his international athletes.

"The challenges that come with traveling to the United States to attend school and play basketball as an Australian Sudanese athlete are not thoroughly thought out by the athlete when making these decisions on their own. What makes this even more challenging for some is the fact that their parents are not aware of this world and have a challenging time being involved due to them not being educated about prep-schools and the world of college athletics."

"There are a lot of talented kids here in Australia, in my club included, that do not get the opportunity they are looking for so sometimes they go out of their way to make it happen on their own. Coaches will come to Australia on "tours" and recruit athletes to come to the States to play for their prep-schools. What these athletes do not realize sometimes is the financial and safety aspect of these opportunities that may be presented to them from whomever they encounter", said Manny.

Manny says that athletes are so determined to chase their dreams of playing in the States that they pay these prep-school fees themselves. Sometimes, an athlete's highlight video might go viral and with social media and the hype prevalent around sports, they start taking off in pursuit of fulfilling their dreams and goals.

Manny mentioned that prep-schools are the biggest market for international kids due to them not being noticed or exposed to college coaches in the States. Coaches either reach out from social media or put together international "tours" to go scout and pick up athletes with potential to be great. Some exploit them for their own beneficial gain, which is the money the athletes spend. After connecting with Manny, I also had the opportunity to speak to one of his Ex club players that took the prep-school route in hopes of getting exposure and a scholarship to play college basketball in the States.

"My name is Deng Lual, and I am a Sudanese Australian who attended a prep-school in the States in pursuit of fulfilling my dreams of playing college basketball, and then hopefully the pros after," he said. "In Australia, I was approached by two coaches that said that if I participated in tours, it would get me exposure in the States and coaches would start coming to me. The tour consisted of touring several States within the U.S in pursuit of hopefully getting exposure and seen by coaches. The tour cost about $5,000 and I did that for three years. During my sophomore year, the coach said that if I kept doing the tours, I would get picked up by a prep-school in the States. During these tours, we played in Texas, Vegas, North Carolina, Iowa, and Kansas. I got interest from coaches but no offers."

"The prep-school I wanted to attend was Sunrise Christian Academy. Unfortunately, I did not get the opportunity to attend that prep-school, but I did end up finding a prep-school through a friend who was already playing there. The prep-schools took care of food and accommodations. I paid for the flight there and back which cost about $2,000 each. Before attending this prep-school, I never saw the coaches and did not know the situation I was getting myself into. I was just excited that I was getting to play basketball that everything else did not matter then. I told myself I would deal with it all once I got there. I was just a hungry kid with an opportunity and I wanted to take advantage of that opportunity no matter what I was going to face. My thoughts completely changed once I got there."

"The accommodations were not good and the education aspect of it did not exist. They got us mattresses and placed them on the floor as our bedding. All I can say of that experience is that it made me a man and you had to be a strong individual to survive that environment."

"All we did was play basketball and compete in tournaments. We competed against junior college and National Association of Intercollege athletics (NAIA) school during my time there. There was no education provided, the mindset there was 'I am here for basketball and basketball only'. All they ever asked for before I got there was for a mixtape and highlight tape. They did not ask for transcripts or anything of that nature. While there, I started getting recruited, but what I failed to realize was that my grades were not good, and I did not know I was eventually going to need my grades for the next steps. I decided to return home to get my paper work together and get my grades together. After that, I paid for a flight and flew back down to a junior college named Odessa College. I loved it there, but after my first year, they changed the rules on us international kids and notified us that if you were 20 or 21, you could not compete at the junior college level anymore. This new rule rejected and destroyed a lot of kids.

I ended up going back to Australia and two months later, I heard that they changed the rules back to how they were. I decided that I did not want to pursue my studies anymore and turned professional. I started out in the NBL which is the best league in Australia to compete in. Though my journey was long, and I was faced with adversity at times, I was tough through it all and it taught me so much about myself which in return made me tougher mentally and physically.

I realized that everyone has their own journey and path and when your time comes, take full advantage of it, and do not shy away from it or miss it. The perspective I have on it now is, if I am able to help athletes out and stop a kid from going through what I went through then I have done something good."

Like Deng Lual, I also believe that as athletes, we want to chase our athletic dreams no matter what uncertainty or obstacles may lie ahead. There is nothing wrong with chasing your dreams but, you should also never compromise your livelihood for something that is not truly promised or is unknown and very foreign as you do not know what can happen. It is important to always get the people you care about involved in your process so that they are aware and can help sort out the problems. Always do your research and never play into the hype. There are some good prep-schools out there to help athletes reach their next step but watch out for the bad ones that are fraudulent and pose as a threat.

CHAPTER 13

College Social Life

Due to the importance and the amount of stress associated with the sport that athletes compete in, it is both imperative that athletes experience some sort of a social life or fun. When we experience a sense of pressure, we tend to either shy away or work even harder. At some point, some athletes start perceiving their sport as an occupation due to the amount of stress that comes with it. They begin to have negative thoughts about getting up and doing the same thing every day. With all the stress that student athletes deal with, it is important that they get to experience different scenes and environment.

With that in mind, who you pick into your social circle is important and you should choose carefully. Not everyone is going to have your best interest at heart. When I was in college, I had friends outside of basketball because they gave me the opportunity to sometimes feel like a normal college student and experience the other side of college that non-athletic students get to experience. This included making friends at the rec and playing with them whenever we had an off day, or the team was too tired to hit the gym with me. I would also attend events on campus with them that most of my teammates were either uncomfortable going to or felt like they were "too good" to attend. Yes, I was a college athlete and I had a "status", but I did not let my "status" dictate what I could and could not do because I was afraid of mixing in with the crowd at times. Most of my memorable times outside of basketball came from my friends and the things we did together on campus.

A social life not only provides you with the ultimate college experience outside of your sport, but it also provides that escape that you need when your sport is becoming too stressful or too much to handle emotionally. It takes you out of that element and puts you into a new environment that will clear your mind so when you do return to your sport, you are refreshed and are able to have a different outlook and approach things differently.

Usually, when we deal with a situation that is tough and energy draining, it is important to take ourselves out of that situation and acquire a new head space. The reality of that previous situation looks different and you can mentally and or physically attack it in a better way than you initially intended to.

A social life as a college athlete can provide the "fun" you need, but it can also potentially get you into situations you do not need to be in with your image and the image of the school you are presenting and protecting. Some influences in college are bad for you and you need to understand that. Important people are watching your every move and with that in mind, be aware of the company you keep. You never want to put your scholarship or career aspirations at risk because you are involved in the wrong things or around the wrong people. A healthy mind and a healthy body equal a better experience and performance.

Taylor Roof says, "If I could do it all over I would try to enjoy the time I had as a student athlete. I think we get so caught up in our sport and everything we have to do between all the practices, homework, and other activities that our coaches make us do that we don't always stop and realize how much we love the sport we play, the time we get to participate in it, and everything else around that is to our disposal."

CHAPTER 14

The self-fulling prophecy

I don't think it is ever healthy to hold grudges and forever blame others for unsuccessful journeys. At some point, you must take ownership for yourself and move forward. For so long, I blamed my experience in college on everyone I encountered in college but myself. I blamed it on the inconsistency of the three different coaching changes I had. I blamed it on the culture of the environment I was in early in my career. I blamed it on being around people that did not care for the sport like I did. I blamed it on so many people that I honestly believed they were the ones that prevented me from achieving my goals on the court.

You can be mad, hold grudges, and consistently blame other people for failed experiences. But in the end, they are going to continue to live their lives.

That coach that "prevented" you from achieving remarkable things is living his or her life and probably doesn't even care or know that he or she was the reason for your "failures". That professor in your statistics class is still employed even though you failed his class. At some point in your life, you must take responsibility for yourself and move forward instead of constantly thinking backwards. Past thoughts are not going to do anything good but bring you back to a moment in which you have regrets and unhappiness. Instead, use events in your life to fuel you into your next destination. Your past experiences can either take you into your next adventure and purpose, or they can keep you from entering your next adventure or purpose because your mind is stuck in a past you cannot change.

The self-fulfilling prophecy is any positive or negative expectations about circumstances, events, or people that may affect a person's behavior toward them in a manner that causes those expectations to be fulfilled. How you expect something to be is how you treat it because that's what you think. It also affects how other people may view you and how you choose to act towards their perception of you.

There are two types of self-fulfilling prophecy that we athletes partake in. The first one is self-imposed, which means our own expectations for things influence our behavior. The second type is people-imposed, which is when other people's expectations of us influence our behavior. Although they are two different types, they go hand-in-hand and both correlate with each other. This outlook can be taken in a negative way or a positive way, depending on how you view yourself or how others view you. Usually when an athlete is having a tough time performing or a relationship between his or her coach is difficult, some athletes might act a certain way depending on what is expected of them, or how they expect themselves to act regarding that situation. For example, let's say an athlete doesn't get playing time, he or she thinks they are doing everything right and the coach is the one who is holding them back from achieving success within their sport. Their life choices might be:

A. The athlete might start relaxing in practice or not go hard because they feel as if their coach has made up their mind and is not going to play them regardless of how they perform in practice. So why bother? They already expect that they won't get playing time, so they act according to that expectation and end up digging themselves deeper into a hole.

B. The athlete might play scared when they finally get their opportunity. They feel as if their coach expects them to not perform well, so they lack confidence in themselves. As a result, they create more uncomfortable situations for themselves on the court. They mess up and then get benched, proving the coach right in believing that they had no business and were not to be trusted on the court or field.

C. The athlete might ride the bench their entire playing career because they lose confidence and trust in themselves and also in their coaches to give them the opportunity they need.

You cannot expect someone to provide you with an opportunity you did not seek out or work for. opportunities are earned through hard work. The best thing to do as an athlete is not to fall into the negative aspect of the self-fulfilling viewpoint. You need to act differently with respect to how people expect you to act. If the expectations are positive, then of course you want to fulfill those, usually require you to upgrade and do better. The best take away from this is to always be conscious of your thoughts and feelings because they dictate and influence your behavior.

CHAPTER 15

Transferring

Transferring is a very crucial and major decision that the athlete should consider deliberately before making. When transferring, you need to consider factors such as academics, athletics, campus, and your situation. The only requirement that the NCAA requires of the student athlete during this process is that the student athlete sit out a year when they transfer. Although they sit out this year, the student athlete can get this year back as a fifth year under the "redshirt year" standard, in which athletes are given five years to complete four years of eligibility.

In June of 2018, the NCAA issued two new rules that made it easier for their athletes to transfer. Rule number one was that student athletes no longer had to get permission from their current schools to transfer. In the past, universities had the authority to block athletes from attending certain schools. The second rule stated that division I football players could play up to four games without burning a redshirt year.

Although this makes it easier for athletes to transfer, it can also be tricky. When an athlete is openly thinking or shopping around for a new school, the NCAA rules allow their current school to "free up" their scholarship and look elsewhere for replacements. This means that players just need to notify their schools of "intent" to transfer. The reasoning behind this is that schools do not want student athletes to notify them that they are searching for other opportunities, and then decide to return without repercussions if they end up not finding what they are looking for in another school.

So, for example, let's say I'm a football player from Alabama. If I decide to transfer, and notify my coach, and put my name on the transfer list, the coach now has the authority to take my scholarship away at the end of the academic year. If I change my mind and wish to return, the coach still has the authority to either give or withhold my scholarship.

This new NCAA rule makes it easier for athletes to transfer, but also attempts to limit the amount of transfers that happen. Because of the "no returning after you made your decision "rule, athletes are going to be more careful and cautious with their transfer decisions. The rule might raise the number athletes that transfer yearly because they believe they no longer have restrictions. It will most definitely differ from athlete to athlete. The risk in this is against the student athlete. If the athlete makes a mistake and what they wanted earlier in the season is not what they want now, their scholarship could have been taken away.

On December 14th, 2017, a transfer study was done regarding division I men's basketball. It concluded that the rate of transfer between four-year colleges was high relative to most other sports. The study found that 40 percent of all men's basketball players who entered division I directly out of high school depart their initial school by the end of their sophomore year. It reported that 689 of the players on the list were identified as transferring to another school and joining the basketball team. Only 48 percent ended up at division I schools, and the others move to other divisions like division 2, NAIA, or 2-year colleges.

Athletes transfer because they realize that the school they are at is not the right fit for them academically, socially, or even athletically. Most athletes don't know that there are rules and regulations for school transfers. Some rules include sitting out a year, not being able to transfer to certain schools and conferences, and the risk of having some credits not transfer in with you, thereby prolonging graduation.

To me, the biggest, most ridiculous thing is giving coaches the power to specify schools you cannot transfer to, reducing your school options. Student athletes often end up where they don't want to be or in worse situations because of their limited options. I do not agree that the coaches should have the power to decide where you can and can't go after you transfer. If you are leaving a school and the coach does not want you to go, they will not want to see you go on to bigger and better. Most people believe it is impossible that coaches do this. Yes, they do, and some worse than others.

Looking in from the outside, it is impossible to tell what situation these kids are trying to get out of. Only the coaches and athletes truly know what is going on. Sometimes I do believe that student athletes who don't get what they want right away do abuse the transfer process. But for others, I do believe it is for serious reasons that go beyond just the sport or not getting their way. I do not think it is fair that the athlete is limited both by the NCAA, and the coach as well.

What is the purpose of transferring and finding potential happiness elsewhere, if the coach and the school you are leaving still dictate where you might go. It is not fair to put more stress and unnecessary restriction on the athlete.

When coaches either get fired or find better opportunities to advance their careers, they are not held to anything close to these types of standards. I have seen coaches get fired and find better opportunities after. They are not held to a certain standard and are not restricted to certain conferences or schools. They have the freedom to do whatever they please and move wherever they want.

Why prolong the athlete's graduation timeline and playing opportunity with an extra year that most do not want to take advantage of? I've witnessed athletes transfer three or four times before they find the right fit for them.

I think it is a promising idea for both the coach and the athlete being recruited to be real with each other and on the same page. This will save time and a lot of transferring that is currently prevalent in college sports. I've had athletes tell me that if their coaches were real with them and cared for them outside of their sport, they would do anything for the coach.

"Depends on the situation. If it just isn't going well, why are you transferring? Why isn't your career not going well? Did you do what you needed to while being there? You must look in the mirror first and ask yourself why it's not working", said Candice Followwell. "Kids these days want the effortless way out of things. If it doesn't go the way they expect, they want to quit or go somewhere else. But there are circumstances where it's just not a good situation for you and you need to get into a better spot for your own sake. There's always good and bad to everything, but it's important to look at yourself first and ask if you're the reason why it's not going good or if you did all you could, and it just isn't working."

"I believe transferring is always an option when things aren't going well", adds Austin Mitchell. "I transferred from when I was a walk on at the University of North Texas. I did not feel like I was valued there by the coaching staff and didn't like the school beyond basketball. I transferred to a school where I was given the opportunity to be more than a basketball player. I was also given the role as a basketball player that I wanted. College athletics is a business, so if their loyalty and priorities change, yours can too. It is okay to transfer to get what you want."

CHAPTER 16

Injuries

An injury in college sports must be the worst thing that an athlete faces during competition in their sport. The NCAA and the National Athletic Trainers' Association have a national injury surveillance system that collects injury reports submitted by trainers yearly. The system breaks injury statistics down by sport, type, and year. For example, with football, a concussion is the most common and prevalent injury. The repeated, forceful hitting can really cause severe damage to the brain, resulting in the athlete suffering dementia later in life.

This result is reported to be the most common in professionals that retire the game after some time in the game. Among college football players, Within the report composed by the national athletic trainers' association, 34% have had a concussion and 30% have had two or more concussions. Reports are that if you have a second concussion, even a minor one, soon after the first concussion, you might die. That might sound a little dark and scary, but it is fact. Concussions can happen in other sports such as, soccer or basketball. The reason why they are more prevalent in football is because the sport deals with consistent helmet-to-helmet hitting with extreme force and aggressiveness. Football has the highest injury rate with 36 injuries per 1,000 male athletes. In addition to concussions, football also has the highest number of knee and ankle injuries.

In contrast to football and male athletes, female athletes

suffer up to five times as many anterior cruciate ligament (ACL) as male athletes. ACL injuries to the knee happen in women's soccer, basketball, softball, and others as well.

It is imperative as an athlete to treat your body with care and stay in good health, so you can compete and stay injury free. There is no way to guarantee an injury free career in college, but there are things you can do to lessen your chances. Most injurie can be managed, but most require extra attention. When injury occurs, it is normal for the athlete to react emotionally. Some try and portray their toughness by appearing strong, and others are not afraid to show their emotions at all. There are many reasons why an athlete might be emotional after an injury. Reasons include the injury itself and the pain that comes with the injury and its influence on their daily life. Injured athletes must consider their career in their sport and what it means going forward. Will they return as the same player? What possible future do they have now in their sport?

Injuries cause athletes to sometimes feel tremendous sadness, anger, frustration, and isolation. How athletes respond to injuries differs from athlete to athlete and the severity of the injury. Though all injuries are heartbreaking to witness and even tougher for athletes to go through, an athlete that suffered a knee injury might react differently than an athlete who suffered a traumatic concussion. Because of this, athletes can experience mental health issues. They start thinking about the disadvantages of time lost from the sport, the quality of life while being injured, and the performance level they will have to reach when they return.

Most athletes cannot imagine their lives without sports. The athletes that are deeply attached to their sport and their athletic identity are the ones who have a tough time dealing with an injury and the mental anxiety that comes along with it. Most athletes don't reach out for help because often resources are not provided available. Other times, athletes take on that toughness mentality and refuse counseling seeing it as a sign of weakness and only for those with "real" mental issues.

A solution to aiding student athletes with their injuries is to get their coaches, trainers, and physicians involved in the process. Athletes are going to have good days and bad days. Coaches need to be involved, provide resources, and engage the athletes in team activities and not exclude them. whether an athlete is hurt severely or not, they still want to feel like they are a part of the team. They do not want to be left out on their own to deal with their injury.

I remember my first severe injury in college that required surgery. It was the day after Christmas and we had to practice that morning. I jumped up to grab the ball on a rebound, and so did my other two teammates on the opposite team. Fighting for possession of the ball in the air, we fell to the ground, me on the bottom and my two teammates on top of my leg.

Getting up after the fall, something felt wrong in my right knee. I immediately tried to shake off the pain and play, but it was hard to do. I told my coach that my leg was hurt, but my coach told me to get through the pain and practice anyway. I barely finished practice that day. It was one of the worst days of my life. The pain while running and doing lateral movements was terrible. I knew physically I was struggling, but I managed to train my brain to hold on and get through practice. Afterwards, I saw the trainer and after examining my knee, she told me I was all right and that it was just bruised. I took her word for it and relaxed and iced my knee that night to prepare for the next morning.

The next morning, all I could feel in my right knee was a sharp pain, like someone was sticking pins and needles into my knee. I decided to go to practice early, so I could have the trainer look at my knee again before practice. She examined it once more and told me yet again that it was fine. There were no signs of swelling so she assumed it was fine.

The problem was, I was not one of those athletes that showed dramatic signs of swelling for whatever reason. Because my knee looked normal, and felt normal regarding her touch, I was released to get back into practice. Since the trainer said everything was fine with my knee, the coaches had no choice but to believe it and consider me okay to compete.

Sometimes in certain situations a coach needs the athlete to compete or practice because it's important, but not at the expense of their future health and career. It is not worth it to play or practice an athlete that is incapable of physically performing. The injury might get worst, especially when the actual injury is unclear or undetermined. I would rather have an athlete sit out a game or two than sit out a whole season.

There is a difference between being "hurt" and being "injured". Being hurt is when you experience pain which might include minor sprains, tears, bruises, and tweaks. Usually, when you are hurt, you are able to practice and play through the pain with treatment. Sometimes being hurt can result into an injury depending on the treatment and how long you play on it.

Being injured is when you cannot physically operate in a normal way which oftentimes results in a permeant change to the body and how you might perform going forward. Usually in these instances, surgery is needed, and the road to recovery is long depending on the athlete, the injury, and the doctors

113

handling the injury. When athletes play while injured, they often use other parts of their bodies to compensate for that injury so that the body can try and operate as normal as possible. This might result in injuries to other parts of the body, as you are putting more stress on those parts. Most times, it might even make your initial injury worst. Examples include changing proper form, putting more emphasis on one leg, knee, arm, or shoulder. Performing with an injury can keep you from performing to the best of your abilities and even keep you from doing authentic work.

Time passed, and I continued to struggle in games and practices. My energy level was not the same, but I was still performing to the best of my abilities. I asked numerous times to have a professional doctor look at my knee, so I wouldn't have to entertain negative thoughts. Unfortunately, it wasn't until later that the coach and trainer agreed to have a doctor look at my knee.

I went in to see the doctor. After examining my knee without ordering the MRI, he claimed that I had a contusion in my knee and that it would feel better within weeks' time. The doctor also said that if it didn't get better within that time, to come back in and see him again. The doctor said that I was to sit out for a couple weeks for it to heal and see if it improves, but I was given some days and returned to practice.

During every game and practice, I struggled physically and mentally. Nobody understood the pain I was in constantly with the movements, nobody seemed to care that I was hurt. I honestly got the feeling from my coaching staff that I was faking and that nothing real was going on with me. My other thought was that they did not want to entertain the possibility of losing me that season due to my injury. I complained every day and told my trainer that I was hurting, but all she gave me was a brace for my knee.

Finally, I decided not to tolerate the pain, and requested to have an MRI done on my knee. The coach agreed to have me see the doctor again. I explained to the doctor that the injury was not getting better, and he did some tests. The following week, we were to travel for a game on the road. We all woke up that morning mentally preparing our minds for the game to come later that day.

After breakfast, I was called into a room full of coaches and our trainer. They sat me down and suddenly I was scared to know why I was there. The vibe in the room felt intense. I was suddenly scared of what was going to come next. My head coach at the time spoke first and said, "We got an update from the doctor today regarding your MRI. The MRI showed that you tore your meniscus, and that you will need surgery when we get back. Unfortunately, your season is over as of right now." Those are the two worst things an athlete wants to ever hear in the same sentence. You have an injury that requires immediate surgery and you are done for the rest of the season.

Instantly, my mood went from sadness to anger and frustration. I was angry, but not so much at the news from the doctor. I was angry and frustrated at the fact that I was not heard nor was I taken seriously throughout the process. It could have very well been a simple contusion like the doctor predicted before the MRI, but what I was furious about was not being granted the time the doctor requested and the lack of proper treatment from my trainer.

I felt so much anger in my heart that it caused me to break down. All that was said was, "We're sorry, we did not know it was that serious". What they failed to realize is "We're sorry" does not take the injury away. "We're sorry" does not give me my complete health and season back. "We're sorry" does not mend the fact that you chose to ignore what I was saying because you thought I was over exaggerating. "We're sorry" does not justify the fact that you did not look out for me or my best interest. Reflecting back, it wasn't so much the injury itself, but how I was treated regarding the injury and the steps that weren't taken to ensure my peace of mind.

If I have the ability to play and compete, I would do nothing but that. If you are truly invested in the sport and you love it, you wouldn't want to sit out a game as an athlete. If I felt like I could deal with the injury and go 100% every day, I would. But it's terrible that I felt nobody had my back and I felt alone dealing with it all. The most bizarre and crazy thing is that my injuries did not stop there.

"When a student athlete gets injured, it affects many areas", said Akil Simpson. "It affects the body physically. However, the most taxing is the effect an injury can have on the mind of an athlete. Mentally and emotionally, it is hard for the injured athlete to have to sit out for a couple of days or months or however long their injury takes for them to heal. They have to push themselves through the physical pain of rehabilitation and the emotional pain and the thought of letting their team down as well as the possibility of never returning to competition or sitting out of competition for a long time."

Akil Simpson played college basketball at Southern Methodist University. During our interview, she mentioned that injuries are the "the black eye of sports" and that some institutions do not have the funds or the means to send their student athletes to professional rehabilitation centers for effective healing. "In that instant, the student-athlete can feel alone, abandoned, and not hopeful to re-join their team during competition."

While some athletes return from injuries and can do better and compete better due to the amount of other skills they learn during the rehabilitation process, some return and are never the same physically or mentally. Some injuries affect the athlete to the extent of retirement from the game or take them out mentally when they do not perform well during competition. Such injuries prepare them for retirement or transferring.

Akil's view is, "When faced with this issue, an athlete's fate rests on the provisions that the institute has in place. Not all institutions have a student-athlete plan B. In most instances, Plan A for is to have the student athlete perform at the highest level of competition so the university can thrive off the success of the athlete. When sports are suddenly being abruptly taken away from the athlete by an injury, the athlete becomes stagnate, but the program still goes on to achieve success without the athlete."

Agreeing with Akil, although they do not have a Plan B for the athlete, they have a plan B for themselves. Athletic Programs start looking for other solutions when they come to terms that the athlete will most likely not return. They have their plan B, which is recruiting and filling that athlete's spot. They want to move forward and continue to move in a direction they previously had in mind.

Akil continues, "It is also difficult in some situations where institutions are not able to uphold their full financial obligation to the student athlete because they are not able to perform on the playing field. Sometimes, schools do not have the means to help the student athletes after they can no longer perform."

My rookie season overseas in Europe, I sustained an injury near the end in the playoffs. My season was going great until the playoffs. I got through two games in the first round and was on my way to a third game before my injury took me out completely. I was in practice and till this day, I don't know how the injury happened exactly. I made a move to the basket and when I came down from the shot, I somehow fell and dislocated my foot.

I think that someone might have stepped on my foot while I was landing. It still bothers me that I am not able to remember exactly what happened or why it happened. It happened so fast and I kept recalling that day over and over in my head. At first, I thought it was my ankle. That was before I looked down and saw the print of the bone on the left side of my basketball shoe. I might have had the weakest ankles in the game of basketball, for both males and females. I can assure you my coaches and teammates throughout my career can attest to this. At first, I did not feel any pain, but once I realized what had happened and the adrenalin wore off, it felt like hell was burning right inside my foot. At that moment, the only thing I could think of was having the ability to play again and even walk again.

I did not know what was going on and how it was going to get better. I was taken to the hospital where the doctor informed me that I had a Lisfranc fracture and had to get surgery right away. The Lisfranc joint complex includes the bones and ligaments that connect the midfoot and forefoot. Lisfranc injuries include strains and tears, as well as fractures and dislocations of bone. The midfoot is critical in stabilizing the arch and in walking. My injury was too severe to heal on its own and needed surgery to get the bones back in place. I decided to get the surgery without delay.

It was the worst pain I've ever felt in my life and was much worse than any injury I've endured as an athlete throughout my playing career. I was in the hospital for an entire week and was required by the doctor to wear a boot for six weeks without any type of pressure on the foot and to take a lot of medication for pain.

Instead of coming back to the States, I decided to stay overseas and finish out the season there to support my team and start rehab. I was not able to fly anyway due to the surgery, so it worked out fine. My team ended up winning the league championship and ending on a good note even though I was not physically present to help them. I returned to the States and that's where the testing of the mind started. I had to find an orthopedic doctor to continue my treatment and rehab on my road to recovery. I was still in the boot and could not drive, walk, or do anything. I was also laying around and at some point, it became annoying and I felt like I was in prison.

It didn't help that I was also a thinker, so I started thinking about all the things I could not do. My career was just beginning and off to a good start and the thought of not walking again or playing the game that I loved frustrated me and caused me to break down mentally. Through this injury, I can say that besides my Mom taking care of me, there was only one other person that was there for me emotionally. I was basically back in the States dealing with an injury that was taking over not only my physical abilities to play, but also my mental state. There were times I would find myself thinking of the wrong things and felt down about myself. I was always in my room and I kept it dark. I felt useless and isolating myself didn't help one bit. I blamed God for everything that was happening to me and questioned His timing of things.

I was just starting my professional career and for it to end with an injury my first year was not only tragic but depressing as well. I was also dealing with a lot emotionally and experiencing everything at once. It all seemed like a gigantic load I was carrying on my own.

When I was in college, I had a remarkably close friend, teammate, and sister of mine that committed suicide. That broke me and not having the opportunity to attend her funeral was even worse. It never brought me closure so the feeling of her being gone never hit me until I had time to think about everything. When I was overseas, I also had another one of my teammates commit suicide. I was only there eight or nine months, but I got to know her, like her, and value her as a person and teammate. It was honestly the saddest thing ever. To see the team so broken was a tough pill to swallow. Experiencing two suicides within a brief period of time made things more challenging and tough to deal with.

Dealing with the stress of it all, I had nobody to blame but God for everything. I rejected God completely and decided that I was going to handle everything myself. My friends didn't check in on me the way I wanted them to. They really didn't know what was going on. Most of them were busy with their own lives and didn't ask much about how I felt, instead focusing more on how the healing process and rehab was coming along. My mental state got bad and I had to fight so much of the negativity in my mind and the depressive state I would put myself in.

It got to a point where I would take my pain medication to relax me and help me sleep at night. The medicine helped me relax not only my mind but my body. It helped making falling asleep easier and not thinking so much. I don't trust easily, so I didn't talk to anybody about anything I was going through or dealing with. I felt alone, but I also did not want to make it seem like I needed someone to help me cope with myself.

With time, I fought the negative thoughts in my mind and eventually found myself in a positive state mentally. Some days were better than others and some were terrible. It wasn't until I met Samuel Abraham that everything I was struggling with started making sense again and I invited God back into my life for good. Whether you are a believer or not, God gave me hope and something to look forward to no matter the lack of confidence I had in myself at the time I was dealing with this situation. Sam made me realize that there was more to my story than I was seeing. He made me realize that with God everything made more sense than if you were trying to place the pieces together alone.

From that point, my relationship with God has been solid and I am more than thankful for Samuel Abraham. Without him, I honestly do not know if I would have made it through to have a positive outlook on life now living with my injury. Instead of thinking, "Why did you do this to me?" I started thinking, "What are you preparing me for? Why are you pausing me? What new works are you getting me ready for?".

I genuinely believe that God does not pause you from whatever it is you are doing without a reason. This year I had away from basketball was helpful in some ways to shift the focus from me and onto projects that can help other people. I understand now why things happened the way they did. When we are in an unpleasant situation, it is hard to think positively and try to make things make sense. Anger and frustration fill our hearts so much that we are clouded and cannot overlook the negative and think about the positive.

This little trial period that God put me through gave me the time to understand my purpose and who I was beyond just basketball. It made me think of things I would not have thought about otherwise. It also made me realize that most athletes deal with so much. Our reality is not what everyone thinks it is. It gave me the opportunity to sit back and analyze the sport around me and how it affected athletes just like myself. This is when I came up with the idea of the reality behind the glamour. I realized that I was more than my athletic identity and if basketball was to seriously end for me, I would have other purposes to pursue.

I think that sometimes we go through tough times to rediscover ourselves and appreciate the things that we sometimes take for granted. Although the way things happened is not how I would have liked for them to happen, it opened my eyes and has provided me with so many more opportunities than I can imagine. It has produced for me paths to journey. It may not be the same path I was on, but my new path will most certainly help me reach my initial destination. Changing courses and paths doesn't always mean changing your destination.

"The toughest injury I had to deal with was when I had a back spasm in my lower back my sophomore year. I could barely walk or do anything without excruciating pain. After a month and a half, it finally felt better to where I could practice and play normally. I also suffered an awful ankle injury the last game of the season, which hurt for many months after", said Candice Followwell.

Taylor Roof added, "I tore my ACL a month before the official season started my freshman year. I ended up having surgery the first day of official practice. It was hard to have my first severe injury, especially during my first year playing collegiate basketball. It's hard getting injured during that time of year as well. All your other teammates are so focused on the season that you really don't have anyone to talk to. It would have been nice to have teammates walk through some of the rehab with me, because as an athlete you have been injured at some time, no matter how small, so it is nice when someone is there to help along the way. I wanted to prove myself. Getting injured when I did was extremely hard. I rehabbed for the next several months, but my knee never felt right, and to this day it still gives me grief, almost three years later. I knew I wanted to walk later in life and I saw my teammates dealing with injuries. I didn't want to put my body through that, so I decided to let the ball stop bouncing a little early."

Luke Della reflects, "When I was a junior I suffered what is called a "dead arm." I had pain in my elbow when I threw the ball and I couldn't throw it nearly as hard as I used to. Years of throwing baseball at a high speed combined with poor form and lack of stretching caused my elbow to wear down very quickly and turn weak. I'm right handed, but it is sometimes easier for me to throw the ball left handed because the injury in my right elbow never got better. It has gotten to the point where I can't touch my elbows together because my right elbow has no flexibility. It is also tough dealing with lifting heavy weight due to the weakness within my right elbow. Injuries are tough and sometimes may change the way you live going forward or do things."

"I got a concussion my freshman year and that was pretty hard to deal with", remembers Abbie Imes. "There were some things that happened between the training room and my coaches that made me lose my trust in them. Because of the concussion and other issues, I was not able to compete in our conference championship meet. That was a huge blow to my confidence. However, I came back fighting and my sophomore year ended up being the best year I had. I had other little injuries throughout my 4 years like shoulder problems, pneumonia, fractured ankle. You just deal with it and move on and work that much harder to get back to where you were and just keep moving."

"Never had to deal with any major injuries in high school, so to come to college and deal with career ending ones really frustrated me", said Stabresa McDaniel. "After I tore my ACL, reality hit, and I had to figure out what I wanted outside of basketball."

"Yes, I had shoulder and ankle injuries. Though it was tough dealing with them, it was more of a mental thing with me than anything just to stay positive and not let it defeat me and my mental state", reflects TJ Taylor.

Nekia Jones said, "I suffered many injuries when I was in college and they were certainly not fun at all. It was tough dealing with injuries because coaches don't care when you are injured. You are just a body and they have the team to worry about, so you are kind of left to the side. The dynamic of the game changed because I was mentally exhausted since I did not feel a part of the team when I was injured."

"I tore my ACL twice, once as a sophomore in HS and again during my senior year. Recovering from my second ACL was much more of a mental game than it was physically for me. Here I was playing the best basketball I have ever played, I'm projected to go high in the WNBA draft and then I face a season ending injury. I was mentally defeated. For me basketball was not something that I aspired to pursue post-college until after my junior season when I realized that I was really good. Did my injury hurt my chances of going pro? No. It did however affect my draft status and I would later figure out that the injury would prevent me from ever playing competitively again due to the severity of the pain. They say that there are only two things guaranteed to athletes, "injury or retirement". I guess you can say I got a two for one special", said Nneka Enemkpali.

Nneka Enemkpali played for the University of Texas Women's Basketball team from 2011 to 2015. Before Texas, Nneka went to Pflugerville high school where she played basketball and was ranked as the 12th positional player by ESPN.com in the class of 2011. Nneka won many awards but not just in basketball. Being a star athlete, she played volleyball and ran track where she accumulated numerous awards and recognitions. After Texas, she was selected by the Seattle storm in the 2015 WNBA draft. Due to her season ending injury her senior year at Texas, she retired the game as a player and decided to continue being involved within the game by becoming a coach. She is now an assistant Women's Basketball coach at UC Santa Barbara.

Norrisha Victrum reflects on her experience, "Playing for a coach who did not recruit me was a really tough thing to do. The summer I was coming in to Marshall University, the coach left, and I couldn't get released. I also lost my grandfather while being in college and I turned to marijuana as a coping skill which led me to failing a drug test and in return almost cost me my scholarship. I also tore my ACL my junior year which was ridiculously hard to overcome but I overcame it. Although the obstacles I was faced with were tough, they made me into who I am today and made me appreciate things on a whole new level."

"I dislocated my knee and suffered a micro fracture. It was tough because of the timing as well as how it made me feel emotionally. It affected me going forward because I had to medically retire. Although I did not intend on playing after college, I at least wanted to finish out my senior year and retire the game I love and gave everything to on a positive note", said Tosin Mabodu.

CHAPTER 17

Mental Health

The most common misunderstanding athletes have when it comes to sports is that it is 90 percent mental and 10 percent physical. That misconception is wrong and let me explain why. To be tremendously successful in your sport, you need to understand that it is 100 percent mental. Your mind controls your body and your attitude. Your mind tells your body what to do, how to do it, when to do it, and how to feel about doing those things. Your mind gives you motivation, and if your mind fails, so does your body. If you aren't mentally strong in the mind, you won't be able to compete at the level you might be capable of. You may have many distractions that will hold you back from what is important.

I highly recommend that athletes seek help from a sports psychologist to help them deal with distractions or problems. Problems or distractions that might restrict them from achieving success in their personal lives as well as their athletic lives. I know sometimes we aren't comfortable talking to our coaches, our friends, family members, or our teammates. When you feel like you have no options, consider a sports psychologist. Certain athletic departments can afford to assign a sports psychologist to their team, making it easily accessible for athletes, while others might provide them through the university but not the athletic department itself.

I am a strong believer in asking for help when it comes to your mental state. Make it your responsibility to take care of yourself. Seek help, and communicate through your emotions, your stressors, and your mental anxieties. Mental illness affects those that are oblivious to it and don't consider mental illness a disease. Typically, like any life-threatening disease, if you don't treat a disease when you should, it becomes a bigger problem and can be detrimental to your health

Most athletes deal with a certain level of mental stress and fatigue and don't even realize it. Luke Della, who played baseball at the University of Arizona said, "I dealt with depression due to me losing my father a few years before starting college. When I got to college, it was tough dealing with that and everything else I was enduring as an athlete. A lot of things came at me quick that I was not mentally prepared for."

Sports psychologists help athletes improve their mental attitude, communication skills, focus, and confidence. They also help the athlete develop coping skills, as well as help them deal with injuries when they do occur. Speaking from an athlete's perspective, we deal with so much on a daily basis. We deal with personal problems, financial problems, sports problems, social problems, and so much more. These problems combined, and oftentimes happening all at once, can very much affect an athlete's performance on the court or field and their focus in the classroom. When you have a multitude of things going on in your head, you tend to stress yourself out and lose the ability to focus on the positive side of things and what is important.

"I think there is a huge misconception that college is a wonderful experience and that athletes don't suffer from mental struggles", said Alexis Hyder. "From my personal experience, I can attest to the lack of mental stability during the best and most trying time of your life. During college I lost two good friends, a coach, and witnessed multiple suicide attempts by fellow student athletes. College is amazing but it's difficult juggling the responsibility of basketball, academics, social life, and family. I struggled with the loss of so much that it affected my game, family, and love for basketball. Sometimes outsiders do not realize that student athletes do more than play games on Thursday night. We have real life problems but unlike most people, we can't go to a Sunday dinner with our family to refuel our mental troubles. Because we're on the road for most holidays and in season most of the year. I think that it's vital that athletes seek help for some mental health guidance. It's hard trying to battle your problems, play ball, become an adult at 18, and not lose your mind. Some other stressors I dealt with as an athlete was struggling on the court and becoming rebellious with my coaching staff. Fighting the people who have great control over your career can only taint your longevity in the game. If I fight with my coaches, it can only hurt my game. If I could go back in time, I'd remind myself of why I played the game and the answer to that was my family. You cannot lose sight of why you play the game. If you ever do, try to remind yourself what you need to keep yourself in the game."

When I was in college, my coach at the time believed it was a good idea to get a sports psychologist to talk to the team and enhance our communications skills, as well as our cohesiveness. I was happy that the coach did that. It helped us realize how to communicate with each other, how to use the pieces we had, gel them together perfectly, and figure out how to fill in the pieces we didn't have. Working with a sport psychologist most definitely improved our communication skills with one another and helped the team chemistry improve dramatically. We went through a lot of team exercises, took some fun quizzes to figure everybody out, and had lots of fun learning about one another and what made each one of us unique and valuable to the team. I'm glad my coach gave our team that opportunity to speak and work with a sports psychologist.

When you are on a sports team, you are not the only one that matters. You must look after your teammates and make sure you treat them the way you would want to be treated by them and your coaching staff. Being on a sports team is like being in a fraternity or sorority. These people become your family and those memories are carried throughout life. You spend every waking day with them, go to class with them, do weights and condition sessions with them, practice with them, attend tutoring sessions with them, have dinner and maybe lunch with them, live with them, and compete with them.

They should have your back when you need it and are the ones who literally pick you up when you fall. Don't be selfish and only look out for yourself. You cannot succeed alone when you are a part of a team. If they fail, then you fail. If you fail, then they fail. Individual stats matter, but team statistics matter more. Team stats are what gets you noticed, gets you championships, what people remember, and how you get championship rings. I'm glad my coach was able to provide that opportunity for us to speak and work with a sports psychologist.

Aside from using a sports psychologist for team purposes, I took it upon myself to schedule private personal sessions. They helped my academic life be great. I maintained a 3.8 grade point average (GPA) all throughout my college career, until my senior year. I won academic awards, attended every tutoring session, and also attended extra credit opportunities. I connected with some of my classmates to make sure I opened myself up to opportunities. I was motivated to do well in school, and to succeed in the real world if God did not provide me the opportunity to further my sports career after graduation.

The problem was not academics. The problem occurred within my sport and the environment I was in. I am a deeply passionate and a well-invested person when it comes to working or doing something in which I feel I have great purpose. If you do not have great purpose in doing something or you are not well invested in it, you should either drop it or try harder. You ultimately won't succeed without the proper dedication and commitment.

Basketball was something I was well invested in, and saw a future and a purpose in. Whenever basketball stressed me out, or my teammates did, I communicated that with my sports psychologist and found a solution on how to approach the issues I was facing.

When I got injured my sophomore year, it really took a toll on my mental state. It was my first time ever having an injury for which I had to get surgery. Many conversations started playing in my mind. "Will I ever be the same player afterwards? Will I have to come and start over? What are my chances of recovering properly?"

So many things popped into my head. I was dealing with so much at the time, which made me decide to seek out a sports psychologist to help me sort out some of the sport related issues I was dealing with. I can certainly tell you, speaking with one really helped change my outlook on how I viewed everything that was going on in my life regarding my sport.

The sessions helped me put the focus back on what was important and let go of the "what ifs". It helped me through my recovering stage of my injury, helped me stay motivated as well as stay in the game, even though I was not in the game, by cheering on my teammates and giving them the extra motivation, they needed to compete. It also helped me create this positive mental attitude of, I am not out of the game forever, just out temporarily.

"I definitely wish I would have known how much work it was mentally to be a college student athlete", reflects Akil Simpson. "Because we go through so much change while trying to be the best students we can be, the best athletes we can be, and make everyone that we love proud. Especially women student athletes, because our bodies go through so much and so much change. We push our bodies to the limit to be the best version of ourselves. I wish I would have known the hardest battle I would have to face in college was mental, not physical at all. I would have better prepared myself mentally."

After learning that I could only control what I could control and leave the rest up to God, the outlook of my circumstances changed in a positive way. Just being able to talk things through helped a lot. It put my mind at ease and gave it a rest. Sometimes as athletes, we simply need to talk to people that know what we are going through to be able to identify and help us realize some things we might be missing. We heal when we can relate to other people, to know that we aren't alone, and that others have gone through the same type of things.

"During my college career, I didn't really have anyone to talk to about my problems", said Nekia Jones. "I talked to several people, but I wasn't getting the support I needed from the coaches that I thought would be incredibly supportive. I was also stressed from being away from my family and not having enough money to support myself. I felt lonely a lot of the time, which caused more stress. I faced a lot of adversity as far as my weight because people thought that I was too big to play. I had to do some blood work and it made me transfer colleges. I was lied to several times by people that didn't care about the person I was but the athlete instead."

A cliché in our society is that, if you seek psychological help, there is something wrong with you or you are crazy. Nothing could be further from the truth. Sports psychologists or even regular psychologists are only normal people who are well educated in their field and can help you identify and fix your problems. Think of them as extra minds to help you sort things through, and an ear for you to talk to.

They are not there to judge you or make you feel out of place. I am big on mental health because a teammate and close friend, ended up letting her mind be controlled by her circumstances, which, led her in a bad direction. Take care of your mind, your spirit, and your attitude always. You cannot control your circumstances or your issues, but you can control those three things. It will make for a better outcome. Always remember you are never alone, and no problem or situation is ever too much or too big to handle and overcome. Believe in yourself, your skills, your supporters, and everything else will work itself out.

CHAPTER 18

Pro talk

Roughly 480,000 student athletes compete as NCAA athletes. Only a few get selected from the six main sports to move on and compete at the professional level. Professional opportunities after college sports are exceptionally limited and are very unlikely in all sports. NCAA statistics show the likelihood of you receiving a degree is higher than the likelihood of you pursuing a professional career in your sport. For example, take a look at the percentages and data in the NCAA's 2016-2017 sports sponsorship and participation rates report.

The six sports that athletes can go professional in are baseball, women's basketball, men's basketball, football, men's ice hockey, and men's soccer. In baseball, there are roughly 34,980 student athletes that compete in college, around 7,773 that are draft eligible, 1,215 that are draft picks, 735 that are drafted, and 9.5% that make it to the pros. In men's basketball, there are 18,712 student athlete participants, 4,158 draft eligible, 60 draft picks, 50 drafted to the league, and 1.2% that make it to the pros.

For women's basketball, there are 16,532 NCAA participants, 3,674 draft eligible, 36 draft picks, 34 that get drafted, and a percentage of 0.9% that make it to the league. For men's ice hockey, the major pros percentage is a little higher, similar to that of baseball. The reason for this is because there are fewer student athlete participants in ice hockey than that of basketball, football, and baseball.

Men's ice hockey has 4,199 student athlete participants, 933 draft eligible athletes, 217 draft picks, 60 student athletes that get drafted, and a total of 6.4% that make it to the major leagues. Out of the six college sports, football has the highest number of participants and the third highest percentage in sending their athletes to the pros.

Football has 73,063 student athlete participants, only 16,236 draft eligible athletes, 253 draft picks, the same number of athletes drafted (253), and a percentage of 1.6% that end up making their dreams a reality and enter the professional world. The last sport is soccer, which has the fourth highest percentage of athletes that end up going pro after college. Soccer has 24,986 participants, 5,552 drafts eligible athletes, 88 draft picks, 78 drafted by the NCAA, and 1.4% of athletes that go pro.

Looking at the statistics, the reality of possibly competing at the professional level is more puzzling than ever. The NCAA report counted for the student athletes that participated in college athletics at NCAA-member schools only. Analyzing the data and the percentages that end up at the pro level, an athlete from a division I school had more of an opportunity to go pro than an athlete that went division II or even division III.

"It does not matter if you were averaging a double double or even got a lot of minutes", said Deng Deng. If you are from a division I school like Baylor, your chances of going pro are higher than anyone from a mid-major university or even at the low-level division III schools. I attended and competed at Baylor and had the opportunity to play professional basketball after graduation. I'm currently enjoying traveling and playing the sport that I love." Deng Deng was a four-star recruit ranked number four nationally among junior college players before attending Baylor.

The reason why big conference schools are valued a little more is because they look better on paper and have more money. Typically, when someone says they went to Baylor or Texas University, eyes get big and the oohh's and aahh's start to circulate around the person. Those are the schools that usually are programmed on ESPN nightly. These schools have high level competition and athletes.

Mid-major division I and lower division schools do not have that opportunity and it is sometimes rare to see athletes from those schools make it to the pros. This is also the same reason why athletes getting recruited, want a chance at the big conferences. They know there are more opportunities for the professional life at that level. Although bigger conferences are looked at more for professional opportunities, there are athletes at the mid-major conferences that do get an opportunity at the league, either here in the States or in Europe.

In addition to looking at statistics and analyzing which schools will give you the best opportunity to go pro, you also need to ask yourself what it takes to go pro. You can have all the tools and resources given to you, but if you do not know how use those resources or even prepare for those opportunities, you won't make it.

"A pro gives 110% no matter what", says Akil Simpson. "No matter how they are feeling, how their coaches act or treat them, what their teammates do, or what is going on in their lives. A pro is about being a pro at all times. The difference between a pro and an amateur is the "mentality". It takes being on another level mentally to be a pro."

"I think it takes focus, faith, and commitment to go pro", added Alexis Hyder. "If you remain in tuned with your goals, then you won't lose sight of your purpose. Faith, because you can be working for months on a goal and never see any progress, but you must stay on the grind to achieve your purpose. You must take a leap out on faith and trust in the process. Commitment is most obvious because you must put in the work. You need some sort of guidance and peace to remain dedicated. You need to set morals to live by in order to stay focused. The platform you play on during college, plays a great deal in your exposure. If you're not at a top 5 BCS program, your journey might be more difficult than others, but it is possible. At smaller schools you need to put up numbers and win conference tournaments to gain exposure for your team."

"It takes dedication and sacrifices to go pro" said Norrisha Victrum. "You must separate yourself from everyone else and find ways to stand out from the crowd of athletes you are competing against. You also must understand that it is not all about scoring at times. Sometimes, it's also the little things that do not show up on the stats sheet."

CHAPTER 19

Have I done my job as a coach

A lot of coaches can make or break a player into anything special, and not just athletically. Coaches are the groomers and can influence and inspire an athlete. They should not make the athlete feel as if their talent is the sole purpose of their being. It is also wise that they take the time to get to know their athletes and find out what other interests are there besides their sport. Athletes after college, interpret their college experience mostly through sports and the type of influence they had while competing at that college or university. Most athletes that graduate tend to refer to the kind of relationship they had with their coaches and teammates, performance, and athletic success as a good college experience or bad college experience. Players, no matter what sport, look for leadership and encouragement from their coaching staff. They want positive reinforcement and feedback to see if they are doing well. The problem is, some coaches tend to set low performance standards for low expectancy athletes, preventing the athlete from improving within their roles.

Now, there are two types of athletes when it comes to dealing with low praise and less reinforcement and feedback. Athlete A is the athlete that does not allow negative feedback, or any feedback affect them, and they encourage themselves to do better and improve. However, Athlete B is the type of athlete that shuts down and needs that motivation and encouragement from their coaching staff and their teammates to be able to know that they are doing good and valued on the team.

Aside from personality traits and character, a player that knows their coaches have their back, give critical feedback when necessary and are positive in the end, perform better and have a great deal of self-confidence and confidence within their coaching staff, team, and overall athletic program.

Coaches at every level, have the opportunity to require excellence from their athletes in everything they do. They should create an environment of encouragement on and off the court. Although this is not true of all coaches, some coaches tend to provide low expectancy athletes with less praise and feedback regarding their game. The "star" athletes typically get the beneficial feedback from their coaches and are the ones who receive more positive feedback and praise. When an athlete is having a tough time adjusting, what is need is extra work, motivation, time, and consistent efforts. A coach should not set low standards because the athlete is not competing how they should be competing at that moment. They should always set high standards for both their "star" athletes and those athletes that may struggle to perform.

Your expectations influence your behavior and your behavior impacts your athletes. If you expect certain athletes to perform a certain way because you've maybe expressed that to them, nine times out of ten, that is how they are going to perform. Realistically speaking, there are certain athletes that typically shine without much efforts due to natural ability. In contrast to that, there are other athletes that need more time to adjust within themselves and at the level in which they are competing at. As a coach, you recruit every athlete you recruit for a reason. When it seems like it is impossible with an athlete, find that reason why you recruited them and try helping them fulfill their potential instead of abandoning them and questioning your initial judgments of them.

Consistency between coaches and athletes, is the only thing that can guarantee any amounts of success within any athletic program. I've heard and seen how bad relationships between athletes and coaches does not only affect the two people involved, but the team as well. For success within the team, athletes should respect their coaches and coaches should respect their players. If coaches want athletes to be leaders, they must show themselves to be leaders. You cannot expect your athletes to be leaders if you do not portray that type of leadership style to them. Athletes learn from their coaches and whether they believe or not, they take notes and conform to their coaches. For an athlete that genuinely cares for the sport, they are going to take in everything you say. For most athletes, it's not what you say, it's how you say it.

My first year in college was the most stressful year of my life. For me as a player, I didn't mind negative criticism. The problem with me was that I couldn't take what someone was saying to me especially from multiple people at once, if they were yelling at me instead of saying what they needed for me to hear. I understand that coaches need to yell sometimes, but not every situation requires that. I believe in voicing your thoughts and criticism in a way that the athlete will receive the message you are conveying to them. I was a very emotional player. I wanted to play perfectly all the time, which is impossible for any athlete to do. I would get upset if I didn't play or practice the way I wanted to compete. I was always hard on myself and the problem was, I already knew my mistakes before the coach called me out on them.

Most coaches coaching at the college level were once athletes and know what this journey is like. They should be able to relate, mentor and help athletes find their way after their eligibility is up. Coaches should guide, advise, and fill a role the athlete needs when they are far away from home. The very same things that were communicated to the athlete during their recruitment process.

"I feel like college coaches need to be more interested in the academic aspects of their players", said Taylor Roof. "Not every collegiate athlete will play professional sports and these athletes need to have a way to get a respectable job after college. College coaches have experienced the real world and continue to. They should share with their players the adversities and lessons they have learned along the way to help the players out in any way they can."

As a coach, if you want to know if you did your job and took care of your athlete while they were playing for you, they will stay in contact with you. They will care enough to keep the relationship going, and will check in. Sooner rather than later, I hope coaches figure out that athletes look up to them and value their opinions. The terrible thing about this is, looking up and valuing the wrong coaches' opinion. Those opinions can really damage an athlete and cause stress and confidence issues. As coaches, you can coach, do a fantastic job, advance your career, and change an athlete's life along the way. The motive of moving up and on to better things is the same for the coach and athlete, so why not help each other achieve those heights together?

"It's funny to me because I've been around college basketball now for six years going on seven, but only in the real world for about two", said Candice Followwell. Most college coaches would say the sport itself will prepare you for the real world. I'd have to say being an athlete and enduring adversity and hardships are what prepare you for the real world. It's also important to educate our players on what's coming and how life can be crazy at times. As a coach, it's important for me to continue teaching and guiding my athletes in the right direction and not allow them to take the path towards failure, because if they do, then I have failed them."

College is a time for student athletes to grow. Coaches can either help that growth process and make it easier or make it more difficult for the athlete. It is good to have the players' best interest at heart

"A coach's perspective must take on different lenses", said Akil Simpson. "When you are a coach, your lens must be different in terms of the way you see and deal with the student-athletes on and off the playing field. Sometimes, you can get caught up in the athletic piece that you do not always think about the person that is the athlete. A coach's perspective cannot be worried solely about the sport they coach. They must look at the bigger picture that comes with coaching." During her interview, Akil stated a quote by Theodore Roosevelt that I found interesting and that also correlates with young athletes today. "People don't care how much you know until they know how much you care."

Akil expressed that young athletes want information, but they want information from people that are going to give it to them in a very constructive way. "Student athletes want to relate to the person they are talking to. Once they realize that a coach or administration is on their side and is willing to invest in them, the athlete will then develop their mental toughness and will be willing to do whatever it is they must do to succeed and help the team win. Once an athlete has the support system around them, they are then given this sense of comfort and peace within their sport." Whether coaches agree with this or not, it is imperative that all coaches establish a sense of relationship with their student athletes, so they get the best out of them and vice versa. Do not pick your favorites and never generalize all athletes together.

CHAPTER 20

One summer session on, one off

As a student athlete, you do not have the time to do summer internships or have jobs during the summer or during the school year. It differs from school to school, but a majority of division I level schools have summer school sessions both in June and July for their athletes. Summer school sessions give the athlete the ability to get adjusted to the school, their coaches, teammates, and to start summer workouts so they are prepared when school starts for their off-season workouts. Summer school sessions also allow the athlete to take some classes to give the athlete an idea of how classes are going to be like and get a head start. Since some athletes are required to attend both summer school sessions, it is hard to do internships or have jobs during the summer and impossible during the school year.

Usually during the summer, you have weights in the morning followed by class and then maybe practice before you can go back to your room to relax. Depending on the sport you play, I know as a basketball player, we were expected to block out some time during the week to play some pick-up games with our teammates for a certain number of hours. There are also study hall hours for those classes that you are taking during the summer. When you calculate everything that you are obligated to do, you have no time to pursue internships or job opportunities.

My point of view is athletes only be allowed one summer session of school and workouts and get one session off. The reason being, internships are particularly important. There are degrees that often require internships to get your foot in the door after graduation. Honestly speaking, athletes train June and July, get a couple of weeks off before the school semester, and come back out of shape. If the purpose is to keep the athletes in shape almost year around, then I have seen it fail.

Athletes should get the time and be encouraged to do internships during the summer to help them achieve success in finding a job after their sport. Jobs are also important during the summer because some athletes struggle to feed themselves and get basic necessities they need. With that in mind, some athletes are not able to ask their parents for money to purchase things they need to support themselves during the summer. I understand that meals are offered to the athletes at no cost and are included in their scholarships, but some athletes do not have that option. I mention that because there are athletes on partial scholarships. Also, from experience, the cafeterias would oftentimes close early and thus the athlete would have nothing to eat after a certain time. Some athletes are too prideful and embarrassed to ask their parents to provide them with meals or money. I believe it is important that we take care of our athletes and make sure they are provided with everything they need to be able to focus on their school, their sport, and their success.

It is already tough for non-athletic students to get jobs after college, hitting the post-graduation slump. Now, imagine how much more difficult it is for athletes that have no experience written on their resumes. I can honestly attest to this because I have non-athletic friends that graduated within their fields and have a tough time finding work after college.

For a lot of companies, no matter the educational background you have, the "experience" factor matters more.

Obviously, if you want a regular job and not a career job, most do not require a certain type of experience because they train you. Having experience or an internship does not guarantee you a position, but it does draw more attention to you and your resume.

When I was in college, we were only required to do one summer school session my first three years. The one that was required was the one in July when the team came together to work out. What I did before heading to that summer school session in July was, workout to stay in shape and worked at the mall. I wanted spending money to use when I went back for the summer. I also wanted to build my resume and work on my people skills, so I would know going forward how to communicate and work with other people. Although it was just a customer service job, it taught me a lot about business and how to conduct myself in a professional manner. I took a lot of skillful things away from that opportunity and I still use them to this day. Most of you are thinking well, I am studying for a career job, I do not want to do customer service jobs in the meantime. Well, to be honest with you, career jobs heavily rely on customer service and making sure your clients are satisfied. Without customer service, business would not be in business.

Most athletes are not aware what a resume should look like. They have no clue on how to edit, draft, build them, or keep them current. At some universities and colleges, that is something they focus on and make sure to teach their athletes. But for others, it is something that is not expressed and quite frankly, something that most athletes are not concerned about until they graduate.

I remember the University of North Texas athletic program hosting a lot of professional events for athletes, but athletes would not attend. It got to a point where coaches would make it mandatory that athletes attend these events because they knew only a couple would show up. Everyone either acted too "cool" to attend or too tired to go. I know my coach used to require us to set time off to attend events like this. It's interesting how sometimes certain schools will have the resources the athlete needs, but the athlete will not take advantage of them. They think that they are cheating the coaches or the athletic program, but who they are truly cheating is themselves and future opportunities. It does not benefit the university or coach one bit if you attend or not, but they host events like this to help athletes create connections for themselves that might be beneficial after graduation.

CHAPTER 21

"Making it"

What does it mean to make it? "Making it" can mean many things to many people. Making it essentially means to successfully achieve something in whatever it is you are chasing in life. That something depends on one's chosen career path, passions, dreams, and goals. For most people, making it is essentially tied with financial gain and freedom for them and their families. We go through life fearing the what ifs of not making it, talk ourselves out of countless opportunities, and limit ourselves to one opportunity we think is our for sure path to success.

We start to believe that one thing is our only path to making it and disregard other opportunities that can lead us to that same destination. What I believe is, we do not fear failure but success itself. We revert ourselves to the mindset of failing and then try our best to make it out of that failure mindset we just put ourselves in. We try and prove to ourselves and others around us that we can do it successfully, succeed at it and make it. Whenever we fall short or do not "make it" regarding whatever it is we are pursuing, we label ourselves as failures because we think that we've failed to secure the goal of success.

For example, for us to believe we can truly accomplish something, we invent this idea psychologically that everyone is already expecting us to fail. We then start to doubt ourselves and imagine that failure playing out. Due to this, we then try to beat that mindset, by claiming that we will achieve success no matter who is for or against our journey. For some of us, our minds automatically default to failure and then we ourselves try to be positive and get ourselves out of that mindset. The failures we envision in our mind represent the Personified version of our insecurities.

"I try my best to be honest with my athletes", said Manny. "I try to manage my athletes' expectations, because I know every kid is not going to have the opportunity to go pro. Every kid wants to believe that he or she is good and gifted and most of the time it is set in their minds as so. My job is to be realistic with the athlete. Not necessarily say that he or she is not good enough to compete at that level but take in a direction where we explore why we play the sport in the first place. I try to be honest with them without being aggressive, listen to them and try to connect it with education and the opportunities the sport provides outside of the professional world. I also tie it to real life experiences and make it realistic for them, so they do not have a one-track mind.

Most kids in the game think that going pro and making money is making it. When that opportunity doesn't present itself, they think they've failed and believe that they have no other purposes in life. That is why I stress the importance of education because even with the athletes in the pros right now, most of them go broke some years after retirement because they are not educated well in investing in themselves, and lack life skills that teach them how to handle certain situations."

As coaches, mentors, parents, and close friends of athletes, it is good to ask them questions like, "what are some other passions of yours besides your sport? What do you see yourself doing after retirement? Are you investing in yourself now to prepare for the future? With everything that goes on in the athletic world, most athletes do not stop to think about these sorts of questions.

"A lot of athletes are afraid that they won't make it and fear failure" says Manny. "What I tell them is, there are numerous ways to make it. You use your sport as a tool to get you to where you want to go. If that is playing in the pros and you get the opportunity, that is great. If it is not, then it will provide you the education you need to be able to pursue whatever it is you want to in life." To better help athletes understand what it means to make it in different ways, Manny uses himself as an example.

Growing up, Manny played both soccer and basketball but decided to commit to basketball. He ended up getting an injury that made it hard for him to return to the game of basketball. He then had to decide on whether it was worth his coming back. The injury was bad, and recovery would take some time. He made the choice of retiring and accepting the reality that he might not make it in basketball but, wanted to continue in another way to help other kids pursue their dreams. In his terms, even though he himself did not make it to the league like he wanted to, he still "made it" because he is still around the sport and making a difference with it every day. For him, helping kids achieve their dreams of playing in high school, college, or the pros is making it and he loves what he does.

As an athlete, whenever we get into our sport, we draw ourselves this path to success that ultimately brings us to our destination. That destination for athletes that are passionate about their sport and want a future in their sport is to enter the professional world.

They perceive their journey from high school to college as the buildup for the ultimate success of making it to the pros. In the athletic world, there are actual statistics that some athletes won't make it to that destination. If you do not get an opportunity to the pros as an athlete for whatever reason, the next step is to retire. In the professional work world, if a professional company does not give you an opportunity, you can always find another company that will gladly give you that opportunity. You can always change your career path and go back to school to earn a different degree. If you suddenly feel as if your current career path is not for you anymore, you have the chance to change it and chase your new career. Not everyone can make their sport an occupation after college athletics.

The key is not to tie yourself only to one thing and to keep your options open. You do not know what will happen today, tomorrow, next month or even next year. Have your plan A always in the front of your frontal lobe, but don't ever disregard plan B or C because life does happen and there will be other paths to journey. Do not limit yourself and life will not limit you.

CHAPTER 22

Life after retirement from sports

There's a difference between change and transition. Often, change is a physical event that we go through and affects us externally. Change happens often and something we don't always prepare for. Unfortunately, we don't have the ability to control what happens in life and change is one of those things. It is inevitable and in order to accept change and move forward, you must alter your behavior and mental state.

Transition is the decision you make to accept the closing of one opportunity and embracing the emergence of a new one. It is what happens to us psychologically when we deal with changes that occur. It's the mental aspect of change and sometimes, can be a little tricky. You cannot view transition as a threat, but rather an opportunity for greater. It is easier said than done, but very much possible to accomplish. The most important thing about change and transition is to accept the transition in your mind and shift from what was, to what is becoming. In order to make a successful overall change in your life, you need to let go of the past and look forward to the future and the endless possibilities it can provide.

Student athletes struggle with change and transition when the opportunity to compete in their sport is no longer available to them. The transition from being a student-athlete to entering the "real world" is tough and something a lot of athletes are not prepared or ready for. Most athletes are so attached and passionate about their athletic identity that they believe that's all they are and all they'll ever be. They cling to their "athletic identity" and are afraid to part ways and retire their sport. Clinging to that athletic identity typically starts at an early age for an athlete.

Growing up, athletes are taught and encouraged to put all of their focus and energy into their sport and ignore other "distractions". They are not taught that they can excel in their sport and also pursue other passions alongside. This is why some athletes seem clueless about what they want to do or major in once they get to college. Most lack mentors, friends, or family members that will help them map out their future plans.

When you enter college as an athlete completely unprepared and clueless to what degree you want to pursue, you may get taken advantage of. It is better to come in with knowledge of what you want to do. You do not want to major in a degree that does not pertain to your skills and personality and will not benefit you in the future. It is a waste of a free education to have the opportunity to study a degree of your choice and not take it seriously.

Retirement is leaving one's job and ceasing to work. For most people, retirement is more of a luxury and something that people strive and work for. Unfortunately, not everyone will afford to completely retire and live the rest of their lives without work. Most people either retire because they've accumulated a certain amount of money and can then afford to live the rest of their lives work free, or they are old and aren't able to work or be employed.

For athletes, retirement is painted differently. There are a couple of reasons why athletes after college decide to retire. Some retire because, they do not have the ability or opportunity to play at the next level professionally, are exhausted and burnt out from their sport, have suffered career ending injuries, academic reasons why they cannot compete, and termination from the team.

Although many athletes fall within these variables, there are some athletes that are aware early on that they do not want to pursue their sport after college and retire after graduation, having other plans for the future.

These retirement decisions can be hard, and oftentimes have depressive endings. The transition from being a student athlete into the "real world" and finding a new identity is hard for some and even unimaginable for others. When athletes transition from their athletic world into a new, unfamiliar sports-free world, stress, and panic start to strike. Most athletes are not prepared for this role and struggle to find their way and their new identity.

A University of North Texas counseling and psychology PhD student, and a sports and performance psychology consultant, Karolina Wartalowicz conducted a thesis research study regarding student athletes and their transitional period after their sport. In her research, she stated that athletes who identify strongly and exclusively with that role, are less likely to plan for future careers outside of sports before retirement. They also may experience indecisiveness, lack of knowledge about occupations, and conflicts about career choices. She also mentioned that there were conceptual factors that may affect how athletes respond to their retirement from sport. Factors that include the voluntaries and quickness of the sport's termination, degree of athletic identity, evaluation of athletic achievements, and prior planning for a new career after sport.

Further into her research findings, Karolina said that, Athletes who strongly believed they had achieved their sport goals and were able to develop a new focus after terminating their sporting career, reported higher levels of life satisfaction and body satisfaction as well as lower levels of depressive symptomatology. Whereas on the contrary, athletes who exit sport with declining performances may exhibit difficulties with lack of self-confidence and feelings of negativity towards their body (Sinclair & Orlick, 1993).

This research finding expresses that, if you were satisfied overall with how you competed during your collegiate career, your chances of coping and moving on from the sport were higher than someone who was dissatisfied with their past performance in college and felt deep regrets. It also highlighted that if you had positive self-confidence while competing in your sport and gave it all you had, you had less of a chance to mourn and have depressive symptoms.

If you suffered low self-confidence regarding your skills, did not provide yourself with ambitious goals, and did not compete well, your chances of having depressive symptoms and coping with the situation might be higher and more severe. Therefore, it is imperative that parents and coaches help the athlete discover other interests either in high school or in college. It is not only healthy for the athlete but also beneficial for their well-being in the future.

Upon his retirement, Kobe Bryant gave an interview that said, "Twenty years from now, if basketball is the only good thing I've done in life, then I have failed." It is great to be deeply involved in your sport but when that is no longer in your life, and that time will come unfortunately, what will you do? What other career will equate to the feeling you had towards your sport? I know sometimes when our sport is not available to us anymore for whatever reason, we as athletes, start questioning life and our purpose.

It is hard to go from doing something for fifteen plus years to completely being free of it. I believe that is why most athletes turn to coaching as their career choice because it keeps them within the sport. During that interview, Kobe Bryant also said, "Let go of what was and build on what's to come." To live in the past is to prevent yourself from moving forward and stalling your destined journey. This is easier said than done, but you must let go of your past reality, before you can think of moving forward.

The underlying issue is that most athletes struggle to express and cope with their emotions. Growing up from an early age, we are taught to mask our emotions by being "tough" and facing obstacles with "toughness". That concept works when you are directly dealing with the sport, but it does not benefit you in any way when you are dealing with real life. Until you deal with situations, whether you mask it or not, your emotions towards those situations will still be there deep down. That is why some athletes have a tougher time moving forward because they still feel those emotions they have not yet addressed.

Guy Peh, the author of "Transition: Triumph or Tragedy", proposed that there were three phases of transition in his book. The first phase is the "ending", the second phase is the "neutral zone" and the third phase is the "beginning" stage. Peh 's transition book is a very well-written, and inspiring book that discusses and informs people on how to strategically maneuver the gap between your current life stage, and your future destiny. Guy mentioned that we experience those three stages when going through transition and letting go of the past is not an easy thing to do. But in order to successfully move on and fulfill your destiny, it is a necessary thing to do.

I had the immense pleasure of interviewing an Ex NFL

player Jalil Johnson who played for the Jacksonville Jaguars and, had an interesting story up until retirement. Jalil had a remarkably interesting journey to the NFL. In high school, he was not heavily recruited. He also did not take the sport of football seriously until a very tragic accident made him realize that he was wasting a gift that could provide him the opportunity to earn a college degree for free.

After that tragic accident, he started taking the sport seriously and got recruited to play at a junior college in Mississippi. Upon recruitment and attending college, he played and ended up tearing his ACL his first year. Although the injury was tough, he viewed it as an opportunity to sit out a year and watch the game from the sidelines and learn.

"It was the best thing that ever happened to me", said Jalil. Before his injury, he relied solely on his talent and sitting out humbled him and made him realize that he needed to work hard and take care of himself if he wanted to make it to the next level. After his sophomore year at the junior college, he started getting recruited by some big-time colleges.

"Coming out of junior college in December, big colleges are recruiting you and expecting you to play right away", said Jalil. There is no time for them to teach you the entirety of the system. I knew I wouldn't have time to learn the system, so I had to come prepared. Although I was getting recruited by big time colleges, there was a small obstacle that was standing in my way. I did not pass college algebra in time to be able to accept a scholarship. Due to this, some schools did not wait and moved on to other players they wanted to sign. I had to go to summer school that season to complete college algebra so that I had the opportunity to accept a scholarship somewhere."

Most of the schools that Jalil was getting recruited by

moved on to recruiting other players, or the coaching staff got fired. The only offers he had did not fit him academically or athletically. He thought everything through and came up with a vision of his own. His vision required him taking a leap of faith and chasing his dream.

Jalil took a bus to Jacksonville, Mississippi with a transcript and a highlight tape. He did not have much, but he made do with what he had. He had no clue how this situation was going to turn out, but he had faith in himself and faith in what he was about to do. He knew he had the talent to compete, but nobody gave him the opportunity to do so. He marched to the coach's house, gave the coach the transcript and highlight tape and waited for the next words that could possibly change his entire life.

"As an athlete it is tough because you want others to see you how you see yourself", said Jalil. "Everybody has their own perceptions of you, but ultimately, we try to show coaches how we see ourselves and how we view our skills and abilities as well as our character."

Jalil ended up getting offered a scholarship. He got treated well and the coaches looked out for him. Although he was getting treated well, he started having problems with the way some guys on the team were getting treated.

"They use you in college. Some people would get treated well, and others wouldn't. It depended on what kind of status you had on the team. If you were good, you got treated better. It is worse when players get injured. After that injury, nobody cares for you or about you anymore. You are not directly involved with the team. They usually just go on to the next player and leave you on the sidelines watching. My advice is to use them like they use you. Some athletes fail to realize that college athletics is a business, and we as athletes should also try to get something out of it. Whether it is a free education or using them to get to the next level, exploit them like they exploit you. If you do that, you will not feel as if you were severely taken advantage of. Get your degree and your education."

Jalil played in the NFL for a year and competed in Canada for two years. While in the NFL, he found out that the league was a much bigger world than college athletics.

"I noticed how in the NFL there was a lot of politics. You can be better than the man next to you, but because they came from a bigger school or had a name for themselves coming up, they'll get the opportunity. It is not to personally knock anybody, but sometimes it's not just talent they consider. Athletes that come from bigger schools get better opportunities than athletes that come from mid-majors or lower division I schools. Bigger schools have more money to invest and push their athletes towards exposure."

After playing for some years and bouncing from team to team, Jalil realized that his career could be over at any moment. "It finally hit me that maybe football wasn't going to last forever", said Jalil. "after playing for some time, I retired from the game and decided to train athletes that aspired to get to the next level. Football was still a passion of mine, so I decided to invest and open my own training facility."

Jalil reflects back on having a corporate 9 to 5 job shortly after retirement and how terrible it was. "Some athletes are not conditioned to work a 9 to 5 out of college or in life. They are not conditioned for the professional work world and can sometimes feel miserable working those jobs. Some athletes have a different mindset, and those mindsets do not fit the work field. When I was in college, I majored in business. Entering the business world after retirement, it made me realize that I never really learned anything in business while in college. I did not take it seriously, and I should have."

Shifting focus from his NFL career and his short experience in the corporate world, Jalil talked about the coach and athlete relationship in college and what coaches could do to help make it better.

"I think sometimes kids are left in the dark, and some are clueless on what the reality is. College coaches need to tell players the truth. When the truth is not told, it creates this off relationship between the coach and athlete and that is why a lot of athletes bring up transferring. No athlete wants to stay at an institution for four or five years and feel like they don't belong or that their coaches hate or dislike them. Most of the time, it is not because of the sport itself, but the relationship tied around the sport."

Agreeing with jalil's viewpoint regarding the coach and athlete relationship, athletes that attend college far from home usually have a tougher time with this. They are not able to fly home when they want, to see their family. They are far from home, and all they are looking for is for someone to look out for them like they were promised during their recruiting process.

Before the interview ended, Jalil wanted to leave some advice for athletes. "Some advice I would give and always gave to athletes is, work on and improve yourself consistently. Work hard and do the extra stuff. Just attending team workouts is not getting better. Separate yourself and get better on your own. I think sometimes most athletes are not real with themselves as well. Be realistic with your intentions, goals, and skills and work accordingly. Work on what you are not good at, not what you are good at. You are certain to have more opportunities when you put the work in and it shows. Always stay aware and be mindful of your situation. Watch, apply and put yourself around the right people to succeed and always outwork everyone. When you get to college, you have to grow up. Your parents are not there to hold your hand through your journey. You must be responsible and accountable for yourself."

Jalil also mentioned that college taught him how to survive on his own. He developed an unhealthy habit of eating out every day. He got to a point where he realized that it all adds up and he needed to learn how to manage his money a little better. Something athletes are not taught how to do in college.

"Aside from the negative aspects I experienced, there were some positives as well", said Jalil. "I met a lot of people and friends that I had a chance to grow with and even become best friends with. Life is planned and structured for you and your path. Never be afraid to form a different identity for yourself. I personally think it is all a part of the beauty of life. Setting out to accomplish something, and when you do, and it ends, starting something new and exciting."

Jalil's story and journey inspired me in so many ways, and I wanted it to inspire you as well. He faced difficulties and had non-believers trying to get in his way, but he remained faithful to the process and learned some valuable things along the way. The work he put in and the perseverance helped him get to where he wanted to go.

Throughout life, we may come across moments that are difficult. The goal is not to break but to breakthrough those moments that might attempt to destroy our peace and happiness. Breaking moments are moments in our lives when we feel like giving up because we are discouraged about our current circumstances. An effective way to avoid negative thinking towards these circumstances is to control the specifics you can control about the circumstance, and let the rest go. There are no positive outcomes in being mad or angry over a situation or problem that already occurred and has no solution. All it does is, prevent you from moving forward and finding a blessing that replaces that previous circumstance.

Your present may be extremely uncomfortable and seem weird and awkward, but it can very much also make your future bright. I am the type of person that likes to believe everything happens for a reason. So, when a problem or situation occurs that I did not plan for, I look at it from different perspectives to understand it and get an idea of how I can use it to fuel me into a positive situation.

The reality is, we will never understand why things happen the way they do, but oftentimes they happen in their timing so that our next blessing comes in its timing. I'll give you an example regarding something that I mentioned earlier. Getting injured overseas in Europe my first professional season brought upon blessings that I would have not received if I would have given in and let the injury take over my life.

Looking at it from a different perspective, although it was painful and something I would never want to go through again, it led me down a path of multiple opportunities that I would have not explored otherwise. Sure, my journey without it would have been great as well, but I like to think that everything we experience changes our course in life and brings about new opportunities. In fact, none of this would have happened if I did not experience what I went through and embrace it for it to lead me into another passion of mine.

I believe as an athlete, you hold your key to happiness. You must look at your transitional period as a positive and not as a negative. Whether you are religious or a believer, for me, God does not do things He himself has not calculated and brought upon a plan to get you through into bigger. His plans and purpose for you are far greater than your plans or purpose for yourself.

Everything is designed so that we may not understand completely but will seek Him to try and understand His vision for us. Never get discouraged by anything or anyone, and always have hope to move forward as a different journey can lead you to the same destination.

My hope is that you get valuable information from this book and have been inspired by it. I myself have been inspired both by the game and the people that continuously choose to play it. Never take it for granted and never think that you are only an athlete. You are more, and you are not the only one that believes that. Believe in yourself, encourage yourself, love yourself, support yourself, credit yourself, and always know you are more than what people think or believe you are.

NOTES

Chapter 6 Competition in College.

Carol Dweck, Mindset: The new Psychology of success (New York: Ballantine Books trade, 2007) 6,7.

Chapter 16 Injuries

Jim Thomas, "Frequency of injuries among college athletes." https://www.livestrong.com/article/513231-frequency-of-injury-among-college-athletes/

Chapter 18 The Pros

NCAA, "Estimated probability of competing in professional athletics." http://www.ncaa.org/about/resources/research/estimated-probability-competing-professional-athletics

Chapter 22 Life after retirement from sports

Guy Peh, Transition: Triumph or Tragedy (Texas: Reconciliation ministries international, 2016), 12, 23.

Karolina Wartalowicz quoted in "Transitioning from Sport: Retirement, Athlete's Body Satisfaction with life, Depressive symptomatology, and body satisfaction." Thesis prepared for degree of Master of Science.

ACKNOWLEDGEMENTS

Thank you to God Almighty for the many blessings, consistent love, protection, and courage. I want to express my greatest gratitude to Samuel Abraham for believing in me and my plans for this book and providing insight.

Thank you to all the athletes that participated and are going to influence and impact a generation of young athletes by willingly expressing their past college experiences and being honest. Furthermore, thank you to all that supported, invested, and believed in me and my purpose for this book. Thank you to Karolina Wartalowicz for her Research Thesis on Transitioning from sport, David Ebert, and Majak Wenyin for the immense connections and networking opportunities they were able to provide me through this writing journey. Without the investments of such great people, I would not have been further inspired to continue the completion of this work.

Finally, I would like to thank close friends and family that understood my vision and supported me. You have all encouraged me to believe in myself and have helped me stay focused on what has been an interesting and highly rewarding and enriching process.

From the bottom of my heart, thank you.